AFTER DARIO
IN THE FOOTSTEPS
OF A LEGEND

Jules Hornbrook

MPIRE
B O O K S

Copyright © Jules Hornbrook
Published in the United Kingdom in 2014 by MPire Books
email: mark@markpotts.wanadoo.co.uk
ISBN 978-0-9538877-7-4

Cover design by Glen Battams.
Front cover - image of Steve Davis courtesy of Ian Cooper.
Back cover - Academy Graduates XI image courtesy of Pete Warburton.

FOREWORD

In November 2011, following three frantic months of planning, writing and editing, I published *She Wore A Scarlet Ribbon*, effectively a biographical journey charting my years as a Crewe Alexandra supporter. It was an unusual cut-off point, although I justified the timing as the club was in freefall, potentially en route to non-league football for the first time in a colourful history that spanned over 134 years when the presses rolled. The thought of documenting such demise filled me with dread. My time with Mistress Alexandra would have ended in heartache. I didn't want that. So while Dario Gradi was still at the helm, having stepped back into the firing line yet again, I had to wrap things up while there was still hope.

I read the final chapter *"Just Good Friends"* as I contemplated this project. It was a downbeat passage, as I was struggling with football in general; from the pricing and scheduling, to the apparent total disregard of supporters' opinions. The wider game was bad enough, but a number of incidents at Gresty Road had also seen me lose the loving feeling that I'd harboured since I was a kid. As someone who has written about the club extensively - online, in the printed press and within the pages of several books - I have witnessed much more than just results. That's been the problem. Interviewing players and staff over the years has taken me too close, revealed many unusual facets of football life and shattered some of the myths that otherwise lure dreamy schoolboys into perpetual fanaticism. There was no way that I could ever sever the ties, and the closing notes of *She Wore A Scarlet Ribbon* suggested that I'd always be there, unable to shake the habit. That continues to be the case.

So *After Dario* documents the immediate years that followed the first handover, through to the successful transition to Steve Davis. That appointment finally allowed Gradi to step back into the shadows. In reality the great man continues apace at the Reaseheath training ground, and is also part of decision-making at board level. The following pages are therapy for a hopeless football romantic as Crewe Alexandra realigns itself, finds its feet, and carefully plots a new path. Davis is a lucky man in that the Gresty Road foundations are substantial, and yet he must follow in the footsteps of a legend as he tries to establish himself on the managerial circuit.

Jules Hornbrook

DOLDRUMS

The ninety minutes were up. It was a cold, grey Saturday afternoon in late October 2011, and Macclesfield Town were about to make mine a very miserable weekend. I wasn't in a good mood. They were winning 1-0. Mates Ray, Andy and Paul were heading down the steps, disgruntled with the "action" and facing lengthy journeys home as they contemplated the slide down the league table. I didn't blame them. For me, there was a twenty-minute walk across Crewe to mull over the dross we had just witnessed.

This was one of those footballing low points that most fans experience at one time or another. There had been worse performances that season, and most feared that there was more pain to come. But losing to the Silkmen brought back unwanted memories. Chester, for example, played at their ground, Moss Rose, for a few years during the 1990s, and those messy encounters always seemed to involve a few Macc Lads looking to get one over the Crewe fans. So there was always a grudge in the background somewhere. That was water under the bridge, but we should not have been losing to a club with an average crowd half our own. Throw in the outstanding Alex academy, the incredible infrastructure built up by Dario Gradi, John Bowler et al, and there were no excuses to lose at home to Macclesfield.

The rot, however, went much deeper than just one dreary performance. It had been a shocking campaign with zero consistency either home or away. The Alex lost the first five games, had a mini-revival in early September, and then yo-yoed with scrappy wins, unsatisfactory draws and further defeats. Losing to some of the clubs in League Two was now unacceptable. Some might scoff at that assertion; that the Alex are somehow superior to certain sides. But a couple of seasons earlier, anyone suggesting that Dagenham & Redbridge and Burton would turn us over would have been dangled off Rail House roof.

Even the battle with Port Vale - on and off the pitch - was a let-down. Violence along Mill Street before kick-off set the tone, and seven players entered the referee's notebook as tempers flared. As that cauldron looked set to boil over Byron Moore so nearly secured three very sweet points, but former Alex hitman Tom Pope kicked us in the nuts with an equaliser two minutes later. Nothing was going our way that season.

Macclesfield was a chance to turn things around. They were no great shakes, winning just five league games before they came to Crewe.

Add to that the fact that we'd beaten them just two weeks earlier (away) in the Johnstone's Paint Trophy, so falling to a single goal on home soil was a real sickener.

I flicked another despairing glance at the Railway End clock. Gresty Road's towering floodlights cast eerie shadows by now, and distorted shapes twisted and pulled in all directions as players dashed to and fro. It was tense and frantic in the artificial light. Dotted across the main stand the home crowd was restless; on the Popside around 400 opposition fans started to party. This was a Cheshire derby. It mattered. The season was just three months old, and yet it had been chaotic, unpredictable and disappointing. Beating local rivals promised a fresh start, a marker and the opportunity to kick on. The Macc lads hadn't read the script.

The referee checked his watch, threatening to dash any lingering hopes harboured by the more optimistic Alex supporters still urging the side on. I'm one of the worst, refusing to concede defeat until it's all over. The man in the middle was ready for home, but several injuries, three bookings and a single goal meant there were stoppages to consider. He jogged on, focused and prepared to keep tabs on increasingly desperate men. Tackles were flying in. Possession was all and we didn't have it. Below us Gradi stepped into the technical area, barking final orders as the fourth official indicated three additional minutes. There was still time. Those who had left seats to make a sharp exit lingered in the corner, reluctant to miss any last-ditch comeback. Harry Davis pressed, Antoni Sarcevic fired high and wide, Matt Tootle skimmed the post, Shaun Miller was flagged offside, and then Ashley Westwood watched a hopeful cross plucked from the air by a safe pair of hands. Just the kitchen sink was missing. The Alex lads gave it a go, fought valiantly for a point that would have softened the blow. But it was too late.

BEATEN AGAIN!

The whistle sounded; a shrill blast that carried deep into the South Cheshire gloom. I paused for a few moments of contemplation, remaining seated just like those sorry souls picked up by the cameras after televised games. It wasn't quite a head-in-hands moment, and there were no dramatic tears, but the future looked bleak. The tannoy pumped music, the Macclesfield fans sang along and I joined the slow shuffle down the dull concrete steps. Barbed comments were tossed into the chilly early evening air, some harsher than others. The club's long-serving, legendary manager was the target of the abuse.

At the stairwell, I considered cutting through the main concourse. But popping into the bar for a few post-match scoops was a no-go. There were plenty of sorrows to drown, but I wasn't good company. There were few positives, we'd lost at home - again - and no amount of raking through the embers of defeat would set the Alex phoenix free.

The chatter intensified as bodies bustled through the exits, past the programme shop and onto the roads connecting Bedford Street, Gresty Road and Catherine Street. Cars beeped, flashed lights and eventually ground to a halt, frustrated by the zombies that spilled out into the street, criss-crossing over the junction in a trance. Muffled voices pontificated about the failings they had just witnessed. The goalkeeper should have done better, the midfield did not use the ball effectively, the strikers needed to be more ruthless, blah, blah, blah. I zoned out. No amount of analysis could fix things in my head. We just needed the team to gel. Gradi would find the magic formula, eventually. Surely he would?

For me, Nick Powell had disappointed against Macclesfield, especially after his Wimbledon wonder goal a week earlier. I missed it. Skint and keen to do more with my growing boys, it was a trip too far. So I listened to Graham McGarry's excitable commentary on the radio and swapped texts with London mates who ticked off another new ground. Powell was on fire, the latest youth product to explode onto the first-team scene. He was seventeen years of age, with just a handful of first-team appearances under his belt, most from the subs' bench. He was already coveted by the big clubs. At the Dons' new Kingsmeadow home he tormented the opposition from kick-off. He was still raw, a tad headstrong and often undisciplined, but he was a match winner.

Seven days later, against Macclesfield, he'd had one of those stop-start games, trying audacious flicks and tricks that didn't come off, offering a glimmer of hope each time he collected the ball, but frustrating the hell out of fans and management alike with petulance when the ball didn't obey his mercurial feet. He was taken off with twenty minutes left on the clock. He dropped his head, and our hearts sank. I just needed someone to blame.

Traipsing away from the ground is akin to the walk of shame after some dodgy nightclub liaison. You hide your face, hoping that nobody clocks you sneaking home in your glad rags. After Macclesfield, there was nothing "glad" about it whatsoever. You notice shoppers who snigger as they pass you along Nantwich Road; you hide your replica top, and the scarf is tucked away. They have bags of goodies and a belly full of Costa Coffee and cake, while you have spent twenty quid watching drivel in the cold. You walk on, past takeaways on Edleston Road that on a decent evening push magical aromas into the night air. With another defeat weighing heavy on your mind those Indian, Chinese, Thai and Italian ovens stink vile. It leaves a bad taste, just as the result has earlier. Further along are pubs and more shops where people watch your laboured progress. They know your guilty secret. You're an Alex fan and your team is on the slide. You are a loser. Smug Premiership armchair supporters laugh, joke and cavort from the warm pub surrounds, celebrating the first goal of the 5.30pm kick-off being shown via some dodgy satellite link. You slink past, unable to raise even a smirk. You will now be miserable for the rest of the weekend.

I can be such a drama queen, but losing to Macclesfield was dire, and for various reasons I felt that it was the worst of a very bad bunch of wretched defeats. Sometimes your mindset is such that the football world is against you. This was my nadir, but the alarming capitulation was gathering pace. Gradi's third stint in charge was crumbling fast. A few half-hearted calls for his head had floated through the stands as the players left the field, and I wonder what the chairman was thinking as he watched the playing staff avoid any eye contact? There hadn't been a knee-jerk reaction at Gresty Road in nearly thirty years, and I doubt a hasty decision was ever likely that evening. But it would have been interesting to be a fly on the wall as Bowler and Gradi commiserated yet again over a glass of vino in the privacy of the boardroom.

Bizarrely, the Alex nicked a 1-0 win the following Tuesday away at Cheltenham. Harry Davis tucked away a penalty to secure the points, but a paltry away following took few crumbs of comfort back to Cheshire. Even fewer made the trip to Aldershot later that week on the Saturday afternoon, and those who chose to stay at home were spared an insipid 3-1 defeat. There was little cohesion. The famed midfield playmaking was non-existent. The attack lacked conviction, drive and the essential killer touch. There were squabbles between defenders. Something was amiss. The die-hard loyalists refused to accept it, but a storm was brewing. Change wasn't the Alex way, but many were now demanding it.

Gradi wasn't prepared to throw the towel in, and yet the bad feeling was such that I suspect that the club directors had to discuss the situation - despite the man being one of their equals. He'd been in the situation before, some four years earlier, prior to the appointment of Steve Holland. And yet this was different; if it happened there would be finality to accompany any decision to shunt him aside. The visionary coach would be parked down a siding and isolated with no chance of another comeback. That's how we saw it. So his comments to the press that week were fascinating, effectively stating that he would decide when the time was right to step down, not the fans. He was still very much in charge, whether we liked it or not!

That self-confidence, belief and what some would call arrogance always endeared me to Gradi. He was never an overbearing manager, someone who craved media attention or adulation from the fans. But from June 1983, when he convinced Norman Rowlinson (Crewe Alex chairman, 1964-1987) that he was the right man for the Alex job, he had a single-minded vision, a long-term plan for a previously failing club. The Crewe supporters soon realised that he was right, closely followed by the other lower league chairmen who initially laughed at his long contract offers. Finally the giants of the top flight joined the appreciation society as more and more of his players rose to the summit of the English game. It took time but he got it right, and on a shoestring budget. And for the record, a rough estimate of cash received for players developed and improved by Gradi since he arrived at Crewe (through to 2014) is… drum roll… about thirty two million pounds!

So to the next match that attracted just 3,521 supporters to Gresty Road. That was the bare bones, supplemented by a handful from the South West coast. I was already depressed when Torquay United came to visit on Saturday 5th November. On that miserable Guy Fawkes afternoon we were in desperate need of entertainment, something to offer a glimmer of hope. But the fireworks that started at 3:09pm celebrated a snatched lead for the Gulls, largely against the run of play.

WE WANT GRADI OUT!

We had heard it before, but not so early in a game. That in itself was embarrassing, and the modest numbers from Devon revelled in our discomfort. The Alex rallied, launched a few promising moves but fell short in front of goal. That had been a common theme for some time. As a unit we still did the right things, kept possession and made the opposition look second best. And yet, ask any football historian which statistic matters the most. It's the black and white score line, recorded in end-of-season reviews, at the Football League headquarters, and these days online for the whole world to see.

Into the second half we still trailed. There was no sign of a change from Gradi. The crowd became increasingly restless, and then hostile when Torquay slammed another past Steve Phillips. "You don't know what you're doing" boomed the disgruntled fans behind the goal. They were joined by pockets of supporters in the main stand. It was now uncomfortable, almost intimidating. But still no changes, even with young Powell on the bench, a creative player that might unlock the opposition's defence.

STILL NO SUBSTITUTIONS!

Fifteen minutes later, with supporters increasingly on the Alex players' backs, Torquay's third hit the net. Game over, with twenty minutes still remaining. Even the stadium announcer muttered the scorer's name in hushed tones. He didn't want to rub salt in the wounds. It was bad enough watching a decent five-minute spell of possession end with a solid tackle, quick one-two and a break-away move that resulted in the ball beating the Alex goalkeeper - again.

And then Gradi reacted. On came Powell and Sarcevic, fresh legs to chase a game that was already lost. There was widespread condemnation from the seats. It was all too late, typical Gradi giving his substitutes no time to make an impact. What was the point? The attendance at this point must have been sub-3,000 as hundreds had flocked out when the third goal went in. The manager returned to his seat. The Alex technical area was empty. We'd run out of ideas.

It was as though he'd had enough himself and decided to drive the Alex into the ground. Nobody else could have what he created. He was taking his ball home. What a ridiculous notion, but that's how it felt as he appeared to be clinging on to retain control of "his" club. It probably wasn't like that; Gradi never sought power. He always did what he thought was right. He made changes if he thought they would make a difference. Players would only be brought into the club if they were better than our own. And as an accomplished manager, he must have looked at some from other clubs stood on the touchline alongside him and wondered how they'd passed coaching badges, how they had sweet-talked chairmen to get their job. I'm not saying he was pompous or snobbish about others, but by now Gradi was football royalty. To some he was untouchable.

He walked off the pitch that afternoon, the famous stoop, muttering, analysing the ground as he went, frowning, thinking but showing little emotion as he made his way to the dressing room. It was an awful situation, but one that had been festering for some time. We were livid; but I bet it tormented him just the same. The man who had always found the right answers looked as though he'd run out of ideas.

A SORRY SAGA

She Wore A Scarlet Ribbon touched upon the commotion at Crewe, but didn't really do it justice. In the cold light of day there was much to consider. A number of snippets have emerged about the turmoil that engulfed the club over several turbulent seasons. It's apparent that all concerned were desperate to make the right decisions; but there was a fear of getting it wrong. Nobody knew how to deal with the upheaval. There were a number of alleged problems that seemed to have an impact on the players. As supporters, we looked on in utter disbelief, impatient to move on but terrified that our beloved club was going to get sucked down. We didn't have all of the information, but from the outside it looked hopeless.

We are a reactionary bunch - fickle, hopeful, pessimistic and yet passionate. Few other sports or industries engender such fierce emotions. The outcome of games, the appointment of leaders and the way our clubs are perceived matter more than life or death - at least to some of us. Crewe Alexandra had been dragged backwards through a thorny hedge and it hurt like hell. It needed fixing properly, and no amount of sticking plasters would suffice. We'd tried that, and failed. By way of a recap, here's a potted history of the dark days that took us to the abyss, a somewhat dramatic angle but one adopted by football fans the world over.

First, there was Steve Holland. He always was the man destined to succeed Dario Gradi. That was never a secret. He was unknown to the wider football community, just a decent coach who had been instrumental in shaping future Alex stars who would go on to shine bright in the higher divisions. Everyone thought his promotion was the right decision. It was along the lines of the Liverpool boot-room philosophy, a production line of coaches and managers to mirror what happened out on the academy training pitches. He was a great fit. Ahead of the summer of 2007, Holland became first-team coach and Gradi was made Technical Director, whatever that means.

Therein lay our first conundrum: what actually changed? The Alex had a system that worked, or at least operated successfully for over two decades. Now they attempted to change the structure. Someone, perhaps Gradi, wanted to adopt the mainland European penchant for using a coach with an overseeing director of football. The Alex had evolved substantially across the years, moving on from the dour image associated with the club's lowest point of the late 1970s and early 1980s. But we were no cosmopolitan organisation. This was Gresty Road, sat next to a railway hub in what was a blue collar town. Cappuccinos were not readily available from the pie hut, and the Corner Bar was still more Carlsberg than cocktails. It seemed strange that the management wanted to embrace Euro culture.

Still, we played along with the ruse. Holland's first game was a triumph, a 2-1 home win over Brighton at the start of the 2007/08 season. Gary Roberts' two penalties did the trick, but there was little magic across the next nine months. What started so well and seemed to be the perfect transition deteriorated quickly. Nobody wanted him to fail, but Holland's tenure quickly became a shambles. When the Alex won only one of the next twelve matches, everyone realised that filling Gradi's boots was going to be a large step too far for the young pretender. He was a behind-the-scenes coach, an analyst, but not a front-of-house manager.

Only a mid-season blitz of decent wins saved his bacon during that handover campaign, as what followed caused Alex hearts to miss a beat. Holland failed to find the right formula and watched his side win just four of the last fourteen matches, and his first season ended with a shocking 4-1 reverse at home to Oldham Athletic. Amazingly, with fifty points on the board, the Alex avoided relegation by a whisker. Most concerning was that the squad boasted experience and quality. Young striker Nicky Maynard was hitting top form, flying winger Steve Jones was back on loan, as was midfield maestro Kenny Lunt, and vastly experienced Neil Cox was marshalling the defence. The lack of form suggested that the manager's team selections were wrong, that his pre-match talks were uninspiring, or that he did not adapt to games with appropriate tactical changes. Something was definitely amiss.

If that was the wake-up call, Holland failed to set his alarm for the new season. A flurry of transfer activity bemused supporters as the former academy leader brought in relatively unknown players to shake things up. His actions certainly did that, with uncertainty sweeping through the fan base. In fact, for the first time since the early Championship days the Alex chequebook flexed to the tune of £1m. In came John Brayford, Calvin Zola, Joel Grant, Steve Collis, Clayton Donaldson and Anthony Elding over a period of substantial change. But what had happened in the space of twelve months to encourage him to deviate from the club's core ethos so dramatically? Moreover, with Gradi still in the background, why didn't he keep his apprentice on the right path? Or was he also 100% behind the new-look squad?

The second season did not start well. Bizarrely paired with Brighton yet again on the opening day, this time Holland's men fell short.

Calvin Zola, one of his new strikers, grabbed the Alex goal, but a 2-1 defeat was a warning. Over the next few months, inconsistency reigned supreme and a torrid winless streak was too much for both supporters and the Alex board.

For me the enduring memory of this awful phase was the home-painted banners and a pocket of vocal supporters high up in the main stand against Peterborough in late October 2008. The reality was that the majority wanted the club to act, but couldn't bring themselves to join the rebels. The numbers involved were increasing, especially on that foggy Tuesday night as we looked for the first win in ten games. There had already been remonstrations, but to garner maximum exposure and publicity for the "*Holland Out*" cause, a noisy bunch of around forty fans launched their latest assault directly in front of the media bench. The Radio Stoke commentary shocked listeners as bursts of song, chants and derogatory comments hung heavy on the airwaves. The assembled journalists from other stations and newspapers didn't know what to make of it. It was gold dust copy to them...

ALEX ON THE BRINK!

Tom Pope didn't quite save the "night", but his late leveller against Posh to scrape a draw prevented the scenes turning ugly. The result wasn't much, and the Alex remained bottom of the league on a paltry nine points. The cheers that greeted the goal were more jeers, but most traipsed home to drown sorrows with a mug of hot chocolate - or something much stronger. A few hung around and continued to protest, their demands echoing around eerily empty stands. It wasn't pleasant, and during my supporting life I'd only heard and seen similar back in the early 1980s when Norman Rowlinson was lambasted by the disgruntled masses who took to the pitch to let off steam. It wasn't that bad for Holland, there was no uprising, but he heard every one of the insults thrown at the technical area. And the method of attack had evolved. The Internet was by now a breeding ground for hate, and keyboard warriors besmirched his authority mercilessly. Sadly, the beleaguered manager's family was also targeted (unforgivable, by the way) and the various social media streams were the perfect platform for vitriol and negativity. If he sneezed he was accused of spreading cold. If a player disappointed on the pitch it was his fault, not Gradi's (who in some cases had probably been equally responsible for the acquisitions) or even John Bowler (who will have sanctioned any deals). Holland was the unwitting fall guy.

He made mistakes, for sure, and of the rash signings midway through his tenure perhaps only Clayton Donaldson eventually flourished and continued to progress when he moved on to pastures new (to Brentford in July 2011). The lanky striker didn't deliver for the man who bought him, but across his 117 Alex appearances he racked up 47 goals. Impressive, but it took Gradi and, later, Gudjon Thordarson to get the best from the forward. Under Holland, he scored three goals.

John Brayford also moved on for good money (to Derby, alongside Crewe Alex academy product James Bailey), but the rest of Holland's squad additions were average at best. For a club renowned for developing its own it had been a departure too far. Perhaps if the team he attempted to manufacture had flirted around the play-off zone, beaten Liverpool in the League Cup (we lost at Anfield) or maintained a decent home record, then he would have been given more time. It just wasn't to be.

In mid-November 2008 he was moved aside. The Alex had fallen yet again, this time to lowly Leyton Orient. It was too much for the fans. The majority (and it was by now) joined chants for him to go as the players left the field following a miserable 2-0 defeat. Holland stubbornly refused to quit and claimed that his side were close to turning things around. That wasn't enough, and the board finally acted. The Holland stint had dragged on, and on. His failure was the club's failure, and they knew that. So it had to be done, but there was no bloodshed. Holland wasn't sacked, rather removed from his role.

ONLY AT THE ALEX!

Fittingly, there was no kerfuffle at Gresty Road. There was no PR blitz. The media didn't camp outside the ground hungry for column inches. The club would, it announced, look at Holland's role within the wider set-up. Few believed that it would work, especially after the dreadful abuse he endured in his final days as first team coach. Sure enough, just one month later it was obvious that he couldn't continue at Crewe - in any capacity. So he won further admirers (joke) by moving to Stoke City to head up their academy, before joining Chelsea in August 2009. Years later, it's still a bizarre sight watching Holland alongside various world-famous managers on the Stamford Bridge bench. He still clutches his clipboard (or is it a tablet computer these days?), still analyses the game, and still nudges the gaffer (latterly Jose Mourinho) when he has a nugget of information that he believes will help transform the play out on the pitch. He is obviously a well-respected coach; perhaps not cut out to manage.

This is where the comedian delivers his killer gag. We were floundering, unsure whether to revert to Gradi full-time or trawl the managerial CVs for someone who would slot straight into the cosy Gresty

Road family. The Alex needed a man who understood youth, championed pure football and had no demands for a blank chequebook. There was a shortlist of none. Instead, Gradi took control while other avenues were explored. Sometime later, John Bowler told me that Gradi had never wanted to resume first-team duties. I recall thinking that Gradi probably enjoyed being Mr Dependable, the man that Crewe Alexandra HAD to turn to. I was wrong.

Another great quote emphasised how important the academy was: 'The man who comes in needs to be one who wants to keep a youth scheme. It can't be a short term fix, it must be long term,' was the message put out to the media. It was reassuring that the club didn't want a quickie solution. But when the favourite for the job emerged I wondered if the chairman had been led up a blind alley. The appointment of Gudjon Thordarson on Christmas Eve 2008 was, to say the least, a surprise. I'd hoped for an elegant present, wrapped with a bow and sprinkled with stardust; we got a brash Icelander huffing and puffing on a party blower. What were they thinking? The mould wasn't just broken; the Crewe Alexandra ethos was shattered into a thousand pieces.

Okay, so Thordarson came with references. He'd done a decent job with Stoke City (therein lies problem number one, an association that didn't sit well with many Alex fans), he'd managed the Iceland national side, and he was shouty, motivational and demanded a fit squad - everything Gradi and Holland were not. It was a major departure, a trip into the unknown. Fans shook heads, contemplated more disruption and envisaged a clear-out on many levels. But this was football, a results-driven game. If Thordarson could get us back into the Championship he would join the Gresty Road hall of fame. A winning team always appeases even the most critical, but it was a lot to ask of the new man. He had no chance.

Perhaps my disparaging prose gives it away, but Thordarson was a non-starter - at least as far as many Crewe fans were concerned. We gave him a few months, tolerated the alleged behind-the-scenes fall-outs, rumours of friction with Gradi, and enjoyed a few wins thanks to his "blend" of football. The man even collected "*Manager of the Month*" for February 2009. Things looked up, briefly. When spring arrived we expected mild weather and a pleasant summer ahead. Instead there was another downpour. It rained hard on the Alex from March until early May. Our charge up the League One table levelled off and it was all downhill thereafter. He talked tough, told us we'd fight to the death and spoke about the future. But Thordarson's appointment was a mistake in my opinion, and it was just a question of when the Alex hierarchy would admit it. They recruited him in good faith, but what he delivered was far from their original remit.

Through all of this, from the drawn-out affair involving Holland to the strange appointment of Thordarson, I think back to how the Crewe chairman held up. It must have been agony for the man. This was not how he planned things; those hopeful, lengthy discussions with Gradi and fellow board members as they mapped out the next ten years counted for nothing. The club had been a beacon of hope for other lower-league outfits, a model from which they could take inspiration from. Now it was failing. It was hard enough balancing the books, so the last thing that Bowler needed was another management headache. Gradi had always looked after that department. This was new territory for the chairman, a former pharmaceuticals man, perhaps unaccustomed to rapid change. He had other issues to contend with, as a boardroom battle of sorts was developing in the background. Where the men in suits had previously pulled together, the first cracks were also forming that threatened to split lifelong friendships and business partnerships. Club shares, overall ownership and control, plus the creation of convoluted new companies beneath the club's core name caused supporters concern. And under the stand, after certain matches, Bowler looked ashen when he tried to put on a brave face for the fans. He was fighting to keep the club on a steady course while the manager put out fires on the pitch.

So there was a weird acceptance of relegation when the Alex lost to Stockport County on a Friday night in April. The penultimate game, it was the last opportunity to save a tepid season and keep the club clear of League Two. It had been over a decade since we'd last played in the bottom division. Nobody wanted it, and tolerating Thordarson's "style" was a small price if he could pull off a great escape at the eleventh hour. And I genuinely mean that. We had wanted Holland to prosper, and we wanted Thordarson to prosper. We wanted Crewe Alexandra to prosper. Neither of the new managers delivered.

By now, even the most casual Crewe Alexandra observer would realise that rash sackings were not a regular feature on the club's annual calendar. It's about the bigger picture. Few were keen on Thordarson, but I don't think we could pin all of our ongoing woes on his back. Chairmen often rankle, players are despised and managers can drive supporters mad with pathetic post-match excuses and incomprehensible tactics. But you plod on as long as the club is okay. You support "the

Alex", not the characters that will have moved on before too long. Giving the gaffer's armband to a non-believer was a bold, daft and somewhat random move, but in true Crewe style there was no axe wielded during the summer after that relegation.

Perhaps they [the board] should have taken action, as the Iceman failed to resurrect fortunes in the first half of the following campaign. He'd done more than okay with our A500 rivals Stoke City years earlier, but with a lesser squad and mere petty cash resources I believe that he was found out. The Alex floundered and never looked likely to set League Two alight. He lasted twelve games into the 2009/10 season, and defeat to Bury (2-3) was the straw that broke the impostor camel's back. The board decided that enough was enough, and this time there was a somewhat determined and forthright statement issued by the club. Thordarson was sacked, no messing.

GRADI'S THIRD COMING!

At the time, I remember reading the chairman's words with caution and a little concern. The club was, he said, fortunate to have the experience of Gradi to call upon in our time of need. That was fair enough. We were lucky. Other lower league clubs would have jumped at the chance to have the man overseeing their team. What Bowler also said was fascinating. Our hunt for a new leader would not be rushed. The club had to find a "longer-term successor". We needed to promote and develop our managers just as we did with players. So the next appointment would come from within, that was the immediate assumption. But when, and who did he mean? The underlying message was that Gradi was back to stay, certainly for the foreseeable future.

The Alex fan base, naturally, started second guessing the chairman. We all knew that Steve Davis was at the club, operating as Thordarson's assistant since the summer. Was that the Iceman's decision alone, or had Bowler also wanted the former defender back at Gresty Road as part of that "longer-term" plan? Davis had dominated local headlines with incredible success at nearby Nantwich Town, so it was no surprise that he had been brought into the club. But could he make the huge step to league management? What concerned me was the present. Davis had worked alongside Thordarson during an unsuccessful period. He'd lost the winning feeling built up at Nantwich. Why would he do any better on his own?

There were others, of course, players and coaches working as part of the backroom staff. James Collins (a former player, 1997-2000) was mentioned by many supporters as a potential candidate. He was bang up to date, qualified to the hilt, on board with everything that Gradi had preached for decades. Perhaps the internal promotion would see him in the frame?

So we were back at square one, Gradi in the saddle and languishing in the lower reaches of League Two. That's where it all started back in 1983. That sounds very hum-drum, as though we'd gone full circle and achieved nothing. To be honest, although we had enjoyed some great - no, incredible - years in between, we had gone full circle. Most annoying was the fact that the fall from grace perhaps could and should have been avoided.

In May 2006, when Championship football was taken from us, that's when the change should have occurred. Not a year later. Holland should have inherited the players that were used to the higher level, not picked up scraps further down the line. We needed a fresh start at that point. I suspect that 90% of other clubs would take that course of action. Not Crewe.

The man who played a pivotal role in such decisions was the one holding the cards two managers later. Now Gradi shouldered the "burden" once again, an honourable gesture I suppose, as it avoided throwing another young manager to the lions. He took up where Thordarson left off. The rest of the 2009/10 season was unspectacular. There was brief promise, and of course we all got sucked in. He was doing his best. Gradi was repairing the damage left by Thordarson. It was a handy excuse but who could argue against that? The Alex ended the season in eighteenth position, the lowest finish since the man from Milan took over. But, remember, it wasn't his entire fault. So we forgave him.

I suppose that feeble return spurred Gradi on. He didn't want to hand over - again - with the club in tatters and leave supporters with bad memories of his time in charge. That's probably unfair, as Gradi never did need his ego massaged. He just wanted to produce footballers. But with the first team losing and sitting limply in the bottom division, players started to avoid us. Wages were never the best, but who in their right mind (apart from the odd mercenary) would have signed for a club on the slide? Perhaps worse still, especially to perfectionist Gradi, was the thought that parents might take six, seven and eight-year-olds elsewhere to learn the game. Now that would have hurt him. Having the academy prosper meant everything to him.

There were rumblings of discontent as he plodded on, but the vocal minority was easily drowned out by those loyal to the king. To them Gradi could do no wrong. Like political allegiances, you stood by your man through thick and thin. Unfortunately, this was a marriage gone sour. All parties meant well, but there was no spark. We had to move on, but once again Gradi's softly-spoken words of wisdom placated the board members and smoothed over some of the pot holes along an increasingly rocky road. That's what I thought (and perhaps others), but as I highlighted earlier it took a conversation with the chairman to make me fully appreciate the complexity of the situation. Even then, returning and continuing as the first team manager for a third spell, Gradi would have preferred to concentrate on the academy. Unfortunately, there was nobody suitable. While the search was still ongoing he would do his best to reinvigorate the team.

And you know what? He nearly did it, dragging the Alex back into contention, briefly, during the following season. Ultimately, a string of defeats away from home dented any chance of holding a position around the play-off places. We ended 2010/11 in tenth; decent, an improvement on the previous season, but still miles adrift of the heady second tier days that enthused fans for years. That was the Gradi we loved, that was his destiny, to keep a club like Crewe way above its station. It just wasn't to be and, by the summer of 2011, I don't think anyone at the club knew which way to turn. The Alex could not live on faded glory. Something was amiss. The pieces didn't fit.

BUT STILL NO CHANGE!

One interesting theory was that too many of the players became complacent under Gradi, especially during that third spell in charge. The club budget was never extravagant, so apart from a few experimental (essential even) purchases during the fabulous Championship era (Rodney Jack, Dave Walton and Dave Brammer, for example) the Gradi/Bowler stewardship kept clear of big-money deals that could shackle the club with debt, especially with higher wages too often the sting in the tail when relegation strips those "ambitious" clubs of income.

Instead, the Alex bought sensibly, dipped into the loan market if required (never too often), but largely relied on its own. We all lost count of the times Gradi said that we would "go with our own" as there was nothing better out there without paying a considerable premium. He was usually right, but what message did that send to the players? With a static senior squad of, perhaps, 24 players, little chance of new arrivals outside of the summer period, would it be inappropriate to suggest that some of those lads in mid-contract didn't give 100%? I would hate to think so, as every fan forced to watch from the side-lines would gladly trade positions - even for just one season wearing the shirt.

By the start of the 2011/12 season we had gone stale; Gradi had no more answers. Away at Swindon on the opening day the Alex got thumped 3-0. Worse still, there was a noticeable despondency about the team. Four Crewe players were booked. That was very un-Gradi like. The Alex lost the next four games, and then degenerated into a side that won occasionally, lost, drew and offered little to suggest that the root cause problems had been addressed.

There was no quick fix, no pot of cash to freshen things up, and the next wave of up-and-coming academy kids were still a tad green. Perhaps, but I have also thought for some time that the reason the long-serving manager couldn't get the team to gel was down to its characters. They had become too wilful for him to handle, headstrong young men with opinions. Perhaps they were reluctant to listen to a coach in his late sixties? When he stepped down in 2007 to fast-track Holland, he was still at the top of his game. Dropping down from the Championship was no disgrace, nor, for that matter, was levelling off in League One. That was, is and always has been the club's true level. But back in the basement division, the hurly-burly, rough-and-tumble of League Two was perhaps too much for his refined techniques. Gradi last got us out of that division in 1994; nearly two decades earlier! His methods were more suited to the middle of the English pyramid, and with a little more financial clout I'm sure that his Championship squads could have challenged for the top tier. But this was a throwback, a return to basic football. His "lads", fresh from the immaculate Reaseheath pitches, covered soccer dome and pristine gymnasium were not ready for the farmers' fields and bully boys of lower league football.

A great comparison is with Brian Clough at Nottingham Forest. What a man, what a character, what a record of achievement at one of England's large but modest clubs. Although Forest boasted a sizeable support, competing against then rampant Liverpool in the late 1970s was some accomplishment. They certainly had no right winning the European Cup, just as Crewe Alexandra amazed onlookers by getting into the second tier - let alone staying there for eight out of nine seasons between 1997 and 2006. But Clough continued, presided over Forest's decline as others caught up - and at a time when the Premier League was gathering momentum. In his final season he offered his resignation, but only after "his" club had been relegated. Clough took them up and then hung on too long as they slipped back down. Even now I feel that saying Gradi did similar to Crewe is somehow disrespectful. But dress it how you like, he was there, either driving the ship or sat in the background watching others flummox. It happened.

Perhaps the most glaringly obvious need for a change on the Alex frontline was the manager's inability to actually understand (quite literally) his young workforce. Organising, coaching and encouraging the kids across the various academy year groups was one thing, but dealing day-to-day with opinionated teenagers was another. Perhaps some of the lads who had emerged from Reaseheath were becoming an issue, let alone players crafted elsewhere with heads full of ideas instilled by coaches from different eras. That's not saying that Gradi could not move on, adapt and flow with the changing times, but for a man about to become a septuagenarian it cannot have been easy. Without wanting or meaning to be rude, it's like asking an aging grandfather to understand a nineteen year old. We are talking about a gap of two generations between them. Men like Sir Alex Ferguson managed it, but the set-up at Old Trafford is wholly different to that at Crewe. The Manchester United gaffer had many coaches, analysts and advisors around him. And I know a young coach who relayed an experience about the Red Devil supremo. He was great "man-managing" but, apparently, "not the best coach". So he got others to do the nitty-gritty stuff, technical work out on the training pitches. He handled problems and faced off the media. That's very simplistic, but at Crewe I think the reverse was true for a long time. Gradi had a hand in everything; he could not cherry-pick which tasks he enjoyed. Gradi did the lot. He was/is a perfectionist. It must have frustrated the hell out of him not being able to mould players as he once did. Hours on the training ground no longer translated to slick movement when the serious action started on matchday. Put simply, I think that some players thought that they knew better than him.

***

Back to the sorry story of autumn 2011 and the 3-0 reverse to Torquay. Only a couple of brave players dared look to the Gresty Road end, and they tentatively offered a little applause to the stunned fans still standing there. Other supporters, mainly the younger lads who had little club history to reflect upon, lashed out at what they had just witnessed. There was real venom spat from the side-lines, teenagers hanging over the barriers firing insults. They were frustrated by the men in red. They didn't understand the bigger picture. They were just wounded, punch-drunk from several seasons of jabs that had left the club on its arse. This was our winter of discontent.

We had reached an impasse. It wasn't quite terminal decline, but the club was a shadow of its former self. Above us some early evening fireworks lit up the sky. The unmistakable whiff of sulphur filled our nostrils. If nothing else, that rank stench masked the decay of Gradi's dynasty. When questioned later about supporter unrest, he was steadfast. 'I will leave this club and hand over when it is suitable or when somebody else tells me to, but it won't be because of them,' he told reporters.

Whatever happened, it would be on his terms.

The Handover - Part III

There was no dramatic sacking at Crewe following the Torquay defeat. There was, however, a conversation of sorts. The local media hinted that something was afoot, and we filled in the blanks. Gradi hadn't lost control, but neither the players nor the supporters were responding to him. It was the point of no return. The chairman knew it, large sections of fans had been yelling it for weeks and even the man himself seemed resigned to the fact that he could take the senior squad no further. It would have been irresponsible for the Alex to take no action, and Gradi was part of the decision-making board room. He had to start the discussion.

Panic had not quite set in, but there was now a compelling need to change. For the first time in several decades, there was even talk of non-league football at the Alex. Placed eighteenth in the League Two table, it looked to most that we'd be sucked into the mire by Christmas. If the Alex had been a publicly-listed company, the share value would have plummeted. The longer-term future of Crewe Alexandra was now at stake.

Other clubs would have acted swiftly, but the Alex chairman did not make any clandestine calls to agents tasking them with a top-priority headhunting mission. The answer was staring them all in the face; in fact, it had been mentioned two years earlier. The time was right to promote from within (again), but it had to be handled carefully. Luckily, while the board (and Gradi) considered the options, the following two fixtures offered welcome respite from the bread-and-butter league torture. It was time to get excited about two of the cup competitions. So the awkward and embarrassing slide down the league was put on hold.

The first outing was a Johnstone's Paint Trophy (JPT) northern section quarter-final tie at Oldham. In theory, the team was Gradi's, and he was still in charge at this point. But the rumour mill had been working overtime in the days preceding the match. Would he jump, or would someone dare to push him? I joined Ray, Marie and Dean and travelled north for the match, fully expecting the club to make an announcement. We wanted to be part of the new beginning, the turning point, and the first tentative steps into the future. But it wasn't to be. As we chatted about the prospect of progressing to the latter stages of the tournament the radio news bulletin confirmed that Gradi would not be at the match. He was unwell. That sounded rather convenient and fuelled the fires further. Something was going on at Gresty Road; at least that's what we thought. Steve Davis, the club's assistant manager, would take charge of the team for the evening.

I don't think there was any subterfuge. Whether it was flu or stress-induced exhaustion, Gradi just kept his distance. If the decision about the Alex manager had already been made, then a relatively low-key match (yes, even this stage of the competition was regarded as small change) was a good way to ease the new incumbent into his role-in-waiting.

An hour later the (as yet unofficial) Davis era started in miserable drizzle that drifted over the Pennines. Being a little blunt, I'd say that Boundary Park was a mess. One length of the pitch had no stand, and the car park was one massive collection of pot holes. They still charged five quid for the privilege, before fleecing us further on the turnstile. It was no surprise that the attendance only just tipped two thousand.

Still, the locals enjoyed value for money when the Latics grabbed an early lead. They deserved it, and that awful football déjà vu hit the two hundred travelling Alex fans. We'd seen it all before. Conceding early never played out well. We didn't do fight-backs. Most headed to the tea bar early, bemoaning the club's continued demise. We were still discussing what lay ahead when the Alex levelled through Nick Powell not long after the break. It was a delightful curling effort that found the bottom left corner from a shot taken well outside of the box. The lad looked every inch a winner.

We started well in that early phase of the second half, and progressing in the cup suddenly seemed possible. But it was short-lived excitement. The Oldham players were all over us from the restart, ably led up front by the battering ram known as Shefki Kuqi. He scored the first and helped himself to a second just five minutes after the Alex had dragged themselves back into the match. The hosts turned on the style for their supporters and threatened a hatful. They punished us again with eighteen minutes remaining, and at 3-1 it looked as though we might crumble. Thankfully, the Alex rode out the final minutes to keep the score respectable. We lost. Another cup competition was over and there was no instant turnaround in fortunes. Davis didn't have the answers and I wonder what he thought watching from the sidelines. He had plenty of work ahead, and he was scathing as he gave his first post-match interview. There was a comical call for "Davis Out" as we slipped away into the Lancashire night, but I did hear one supporter asking his mate if moving Gradi aside was the right thing to do!

RESHUFFLE!

When the "change" was eventually rubber-stamped two days later, it was a dignified and stately exit. Quite simply, Gradi was more important elsewhere. There were FA and Football League structural changes ahead and the club needed the long-time champion of youth to lead its academy forward. It would require his full attention, especially if it were to continue flourishing and producing the talent required to boost the first team and generate cash from player sales. You couldn't conceal the results, but the Alex suits somehow massaged press releases such that the outside world was none the wiser to our internal unrest. Gradi reverted to his role as Director of Football, with an emphasis on driving the academy forward as the Elite Player Performance Plan (EPPP) was being eased into place.

In a way, there was no turmoil. Nothing had changed. People were still doing their jobs. There had been no gross misconduct, fallout or player revolt. I am sure that there were late-night heart-to-hearts amongst the key club officials, conversations that questioned their sanity. But it was now all about the results, those painful weekly score lines that were not going Crewe's way. As with Holland and Thordarson before him, had Gradi's third spell in charge encompassed a cup run, or the team had hovered around the play-off places, then things would have carried on. The handover would have been delayed. He was only human, and although he has never been a brash or self-important man, I cannot believe that he did not want to enjoy another successful period as manager before he finally stepped aside.

Despite the softly-softly approach, when the news broke there was shock. Many had called for Gradi's head, but in a very pleasant Crewe Alexandra kind of way. Nobody wanted him out of the club. He was a legend. A move "upstairs" was ideal for all concerned, but reading the club statement was still alarming. Seeing those harsh words in the papers left us wondering whether the club really was doing the right thing. It was all-change again. Gradi would no longer cruise the technical area on matchday.

STEVE DAVIS WAS THE NEW MANAGER!

The transition, however, really was a drawn-out affair. In theory, it could have happened much sooner, perhaps several months earlier in the summer. But the speed of decline in the final months under Gradi took us all by surprise. Even then, after perhaps the worst opening sequence in years (losing five in a row) there was blind faith in the man who had served us so well. Few expected our slide down League Two to continue, as he had always found the solutions in the past. An inspirational young player would be promoted from the academy or a non-league lad would be plucked from under the noses of others. There was always something, and invariably our resurgence would go hand-in-hand with passing football. That was his trademark.

This time it didn't happen, and there were now many factors to consider. High on the list must have been Gradi's age and heart condition. The guy looked physically fit, but juggling so many aspects of club life must have taken its toll. He knew the health risks, and after a breathless incident running up the main stand steps he had heart surgery in 2003. His plan was to gradually reduce his involvement. There was even a fascinating quote on the *Times Online* website in 2007, when Steve Holland took over first team duties: 'I didn't want to be a 75-year-old manager working seven days a week, 52 weeks a year. That is not healthy for the future of the club. I will probably drop dead doing the job at some point, but I wanted to put that day off a bit. This is a better way to do things, to introduce this gradual transition because it will take some of the workload off me.'

So why did he return to the front line, first after Holland and then again after Thordarson? The answer has to be that the man is dedicated, 100% committed to the Crewe Alexandra cause. The quote (paragraph above), in particular "That is not healthy for the future of the club" made me chuckle. It summed him up. It was always about the Alex, not him. Also likely is that after so many years building the club, overseeing even the tiniest details, he struggled to take a back seat. Ever the perfectionist, he wanted things done right. There was never a chance that he would disappear altogether, and I can't for a second believe that leaving the club was even mentioned by him, Bowler or any other members of the board. But there had to be a concrete plan, a reason to promote from within for the second time in three seasons. Another mistake and another change within twelve to eighteen months would have looked horrendous. The turnover would have mirrored the late 1970s and early 1980s at Gresty Road. So there was a reluctance to gamble, and there was a little spin when news of the changeover was announced. Davis had been a firm favourite with bookmakers and supporters to assume the role of manager at some point, but the official line was that impending changes to the academy system finally drove the decision.

One hypothetical scenario was debated for some time afterwards: would we have gone down if Gradi had remained in charge until the end of the 2011/12 campaign? Although the mood was bleak in the days before the announcement, I have only spoken to a handful of supporters who felt that the Alex would have slipped into the non-league wastelands. That always sounds harsh, effectively writing off clubs that operate at the fifth tier and below. And yet a quick look at the growing list of clubs that have fallen and failed to return highlights the importance of retaining that all-important full-time, professional status. I am not sure that Crewe would have bounced back had the unthinkable happened.

At the end of the 2013/14 season, Luton finally escaped the Conference division and reclaimed their place in the Football League after five years of trying. Cambridge United followed when they were victorious in the play-offs, scrambling back into the league after nine seasons! They left behind twelve other teams who had previously played in the higher divisions at some point in their histories - Gateshead, Grimsby, Halifax, Kidderminster, Barnet, Lincoln City, Macclesfield, Wrexham, Southport, Aldershot, Hereford and Chester. Relegation would have meant a few decent days out for Alex fans, resurrecting old rivalries, but the drop in gate receipts, TV revenue and other income streams would have hammered Crewe's finances. But let's not consider what might have happened. Instead, we must assume that Gradi would have done enough to avoid such a depressing scenario. It would have been an awkward season, and I am convinced that further unrest would have taken place if results had not improved. But no, I don't think we'd have gone down.

So the *Handover, Part III* was put in place without much fuss. The club controlled it. Just as Gradi prophesised after the Torquay defeat, he had chosen the moment when to jump. There was no pushing. Change had occurred but it would be foolhardy to claim that supporters had driven it. For nearly three decades there had been a culture of calm and tolerance at Gresty Road. That largely manifests itself in respectful dialogue and occasional "polite" complaints when supporters meet Bowler or Gradi in the bar under the main stand after matches. Perhaps that cosy atmosphere has disarmed us over the years? Maybe things are not so bad, and only the longer-standing supporters still recall the gloomy 1970s when results were atrocious and the ground and its facilities were a joke?

However, on a final note before we progress the managerial transition further, I must highlight what I see as failed opportunities at fans' forums and AGMs (Annual General Meetings). I pulled stumps and have not been to any of these for about three years. I don't see the point any more. With upwards of 200 like-minded fans gathered together, sharing the same passions, all concerned about the club, so much could and should have been achieved. My attendance at such events ended because the meetings became far too tame. It was the same old faces, partisan people but far too set in their ways. I was probably guilty of the same, conditioned to the "Gradi Way" and definitely under the man's spell.

They were, however, unique get-togethers. Unlike many other clubs, we have been given opportunities to fire questions at the management for some time. I suppose the golden years (i.e. the fifteen seasons of play-offs and promotions either side of the Championship era, 1992-2006) softened us, made us all warm and fuzzy when in the presence of the man who guided us through that fabulous period. What frustrated me was that the sessions were all about the football: why we didn't play the extra striker; whether the latest outstanding midfielder would be sold at the end of the season; and why did Gradi insist on keeping eleven men back for corners? They were all fair questions, and it would be disingenuous of me if I didn't acknowledge that other more probing topics were occasionally fired at the panel before us. And yet when Gradi, Bowler or other board members responded with typically plausible answers we sat back, neutralised and satisfied by what they told us. Some challenged them, pushed for more elaborate details. Gradi, perhaps more so than the rest, was always prepared and ready to tackle any dissenters head on. He talked a great game. Within minutes of any meeting, he had most of the room eating from his hand.

Like the stories within favourite novels that we read as kids, I think we have always held a romantic image of Gradi in our heads - even when he tested our patience. We remember the best bits. The forums reinforced this, especially when the man arrived late after a busy coaching session with the under-14 age group at Reaseheath. How could anyone criticise that? He never used such dedication to justify his actions or seek forgiveness for poor results, but I recall several occasions when he put a direct question back to the audience. "What would you do differently?" was always one to leave the room silent. Only the brave replied, and they would be taken to task and their argument methodically dissected. He was never rude, but the implication was that nobody could do better under the circumstances at Gresty Road.

Another reason for my eventual abstinence was that Gradi was, in my opinion, right. There are always quick-fix solutions, but nobody in football circles would improve our lot over the medium term. Without sizeable cash injections (unlikely at Crewe), prosperity will and always has been built on hard work with young players. That takes five, seven and ten years of devotion. Did we really want that sugar rush of immediate success, if it were genuinely possible, only to be shot down in spectacular fashion a year later? Of course we didn't. So it continues to puzzle me why we ever dipped toes in the water with Gudjon Thordarson. As fans we should have pushed harder, demanded answers and insisted that OUR club was more transparent about such matters.

***

In football switching from manager to someone already embedded within the club's system can appear strange. In theory, nothing much should change. That person was alongside the manager as the tactics and game plans failed to get results, so why didn't they raise concerns at the time? If he [Steve Davis or perhaps Neil Baker] had better ideas and something positive to contribute, then why did they remain silent? And if there was an issue with personnel, certain players not responding for example, then why wasn't that addressed? In Crewe's case, Gradi was the dominant force. That's how it has always appeared to the fan base. Not quite "his way or no way", but not a great deal of flexibility. Davis and Baker have both stood beside him, chipping away, but how much influence they had remains a mystery.

One theory for our dire form in the early stages of the 2011/12 campaign was that the players didn't "man it out" when the chips were down. Gradi did his best, what he'd done for years, and perhaps the players short-changed him. Most of the squad had been used to the Championship and even League One, but when the going got heavy in League Two some of them wimped out. Now with experienced, tough men like Dave Artell, Steve Phillips and Lee Bell in the side, that's hard to swallow. In my eyes they didn't fall short, and I just can't accept that any Alex lads somehow stepped off the gas or didn't "play" for the gaffer. The others, younger lads not accustomed to the physicality of the basement division, well, maybe it was a culture shock. A few weeks after the switch from Gradi to Davis things started to improve; but why?

Maybe the message coming from the bench was too confused with Gradi, Davis and Baker all involved. The players needed to hear one, clear voice. When the dust settled and Davis emerged to take his first training sessions and give his opening pre-match brief suddenly everything became much clearer. Perhaps, but as we will see the transformation was not instant. In a way, that always pleases me, as to think that professional footballers had given any less than 100% hurts supporters.

AVOID THE DROP!

For Davis, the initial brief from the Alex chairman was simple: keep the club in the Football League. He could ask no more, as the pot was empty and the new manager was expected to pick up where Gradi left off. The cup of optimism was hardly overflowing in the following weeks, but the fans were content. We didn't know what to expect, although Davis had the Alex in his blood, more so than Steve Holland (and certainly Gudjon Thordarson). There was no way he'd want to let down the club that gave him his professional debut back in 1983. He was a defender; he would sort us out.

And yet he could not do it alone, and having some continuity is paramount to most success stories. You cannot simply shred a well-designed template and start from scratch, and then expect miraculous results from day one. That is particularly true for the smaller clubs. Thankfully, at Crewe there was already one man that everyone could rely upon, and for once I'm not talking about the chairman, John Bowler. When Davis stepped forward in November 2011, the board members tentatively asked about his thoughts on backroom staff. What did he need? It was a rhetorical question. There was no offer as such, no open chequebook or flexibility to recruit a team of his choosing. Offloading Thordarson cost the club precious cash it could not really afford to waste. They honoured his contract. So Davis surprised and delighted them all; the man he wanted was already part of the Gresty Road furniture.

That man was Neil Baker. Any fan of Crewe Alexandra who has not witnessed the unbridled passion shown by "Bakes" is missing an essential supporter experience. On matchdays during the core campaign, or at pre-season friendlies in more casual environs of leafy suburbia, he's a joy to behold. A real man of the people, he's animated, informed and worldly-wise, happy to chat with anyone. He'd share a joke, a beer and a fag as the football chat rages. Most will have seen him with Gradi across the years, and then alongside Davis in the technical area at Gresty Road. He barks orders, froths at the mouth and bounces up and down in his tracksuit with sheer frustration if the players dare drop the pace, forget instructions or fail to uphold the club's good name. He's the naughty to the Gradi/Davis nice when everyone decamps to the dressing room at half time. But Baker is much, much more than a matchday companion. He's the sounding board, the voice of reason, the wealth of amateur football experience, plus the shoulder to cry on when things go bad. He's Mr Dependable, and he sits opposite the manager in the Reaseheath office ready to voice an opinion. He doesn't hold back.

Baker has been associated with Crewe Alexandra since 1994, when Gradi brought him in as his assistant manager. Back then it was all about the non-league that the former Leek Town manager knew so well, players with potential that could benefit an Alex side only a few levels higher up the football food chain. The budget was always minimal, so mining "diamonds" was essential. Gradi often took the plaudits, but there was always someone with inside knowledge working away in the background. And in those exciting play-off seasons of 1995 and 1996 I don't think it was a coincidence that the Alex became stronger, more robust and ruthless enough to eventually secure that dream ticket to the second tier in May '97. For all of Gradi's cultured approach to the beautiful game, there was always a need for a leveller, someone to translate the intricate movement and subtle tactics to players out on the pitch. Bakes was and is that man.

The most baffling aspect of the post-Gradi era involved Gudjon Thordarson. After a few months he shunned Baker, ostracised him and made it clear that he wasn't needed on the coaching staff. Baker was farmed out and employed as a scout - no more, no less - while Thordarson brought Davis in from Nantwich in the summer of 2009 (although John Bowler was the key driver in that move). For a man who had otherwise been a constant at Gresty Road, the Yang to other managers' Ying, that must have almost destroyed Baker. I asked him three years later, and through steely eyes he told me that he'd just got on with it, completed the scouting missions that Thordarson had requested. But, yes, it wounded him, and he hated being divorced from the day-to-day hustle and bustle at Reaseheath.

Now he was back, and the club needed him in situ immediately as the Alex prepared for the weekend's FA Cup clash against Colchester. Bakes was ready to pound the touchline, Davis' new general on duty, keeping the troops in line, waiting to shout orders as required. He is a loyal man. Some might have walked away following the shoddy treatment, effectively parking him in the wilderness. Not Bakes. Ever the professional, thoughts of that brusque regime were tossed aside. He wanted to be part of the reshuffled set-up. He took his place as the teams ran out, fag on hold until after the match.

The same players lined up, all hoping to find form, predominantly young home-grown footballers that were hungry to fulfil potential. More so than the older heads in the squad, the Alex kids needed a boost and respite from the losing habit. For the management duo it would have been the perfect way to kick-start their partnership, a win and a step down the gold-paved road to Wembley that is always so financially important to lower league clubs.

It just didn't happen at Gresty Road that afternoon. It was more Wrenbury than Wembley. Byron Moore set hearts racing with the first goal of the game, but there would be no fairytale cup run. Although Colchester would amass three bookings, it was Crewe who saw red. Ashley Westwood was sent off midway through the first half and the visitors eventually made numerical advantage count. First the equaliser fifteen minutes after half time, then a cruel goal to give the U's the lead. It was tight, there were opportunities to level, but the Alex enjoyed no luck that day, conceding two late goals to flatter Colchester. The final 1-4 score line made it look like a drubbing.

Within the space of a week the club had been ditched out of two cup competitions. The managerial manoeuvres had, so far, not delivered the fresh impetus so readily associated with such changes. But if nothing else it gave all concerned a little breathing space and the fans time to adjust and prepare for life after Gradi for the third time. Even at Reaseheath it would have been business as usual, largely speaking. Introductions were not required and there were no new ground rules. There were no dramatic signings; nobody came back from long-term injury and in Davis there was no unknown "face" arriving to lead the tactical sessions. Even Gradi would have been knocking around the training pitches, fussing over minutiae as usual. So there was no drama, no clear-out or magic spell cast over the players who prepared for the games at the end of 2011.

What sticks in my head is the next phase, the series of games either side of Christmas 2011. Had the Alex squad gelled immediately, suddenly stepped up a few gears and won every match following the handover, well, I would have been livid. Really I would. The fact that the next victory took until the third game (if we count Oldham in the JPT) after news of Gradi passing the baton filtered through, that at least shows that the players had not been holding back. That would have been unforgiveable.

At Morecambe, Davis was fully in charge. It was his team that day, they were his tactics, and he picked the men involved. Well, check out the line-ups and there were not too many alterations from the final games under Gradi. So perhaps the only notable change was aimed at disarming potential critics. That meant moving Harry Davis (his son) to the substitute's bench. Thordarson had given Davis junior his debut (at home to Bradford at the end of the 2009-10 season), but the last thing Davis senior needed was cries of nepotism during the early part of his tenure. To be honest, I don't buy that. Perhaps it was form, or a niggling injury, but it was a clever move all the same.

Whatever the politics and family considerations, there was a new voice in the moments before kick-off at the Globe Arena. There was a different style adopted during the half-time pep talk (it was 0-0 at the interval), and with Bakes at his side it was inspiration and motivation on the touchline for ninety minutes.

AT LAST!

Even then it was good fortune that gave Crewe three valuable points. Max Clayton's 90th minute winner in a 2-1 victory was the perfect "official" start for Davis, and the scenes on the final whistle hinted at togetherness. Just over 2,000 attended, and of them perhaps three hundred made the trip from Cheshire. But it was worth it. Crucially, it gave Davis his first sweet taste of success. There was also another goal for Powell (the equaliser). He was unleashed, given licence to roam and help his team mates to win the game. The result lifted everyone associated with the club and put a little daylight between the Alex and the division's bottom feeders.

The return to Gresty Road a week later gave more fans the opportunity to assess the latest developments. A crowd of 3,591 kept the faith, roughly the same number that watched the Torquay collapse (3,521) a few weeks earlier. So despite the awful run the core support was holding firm. The Alex beat Hereford 1-0 in a largely unspectacular match, but it was illuminated by a goal from the player that many were talking about.

POWELL AGAIN!

At just seventeen years of age, Nick Powell matured that day. The teenager had a renewed swagger, a freedom and wanderlust to poke and probe every inch of the pitch. He lacked concentration at times, but his enthusiasm was infectious and grabbed us all. He was a star in the making, everyone acknowledged that. But how could anyone tame the beast sufficiently to utilise his undoubted talents within a tight team structure?

On the final whistle there was muted applause, suggesting that many Alex supporters were not over impressed with the mini-revival. We'd won two games, but they were late goals. Apart from a few dazzling solos, the performances were patchy and either match could have been drawn or lost. Most fans' cups were still half empty! And yet there was fight in the team. Lee Bell picked up another yellow card against Hereford but looked hungry until the final seconds of the game. He wanted it, and at corners in front of the Gresty Road end he urged the crowd to raise the volume. The first Davis acquisition (James Lowry, a midfielder on loan from Chesterfield) was also bedded in, a clear sign that the gaffer wanted to retain possession and stop his side conceding goals. It also created some competition within the squad.

The caution from the sidelines was warranted, as the goals against column continued to rise in the following weeks. A 1-1 draw at Northampton (man-mountain Ade Akinfenwa inevitably scoring against Crewe) and the same score line at home to Crawley the next Saturday brought valuable points but kept everyone guessing as to whether a corner had been turned. Then, away at Bradford City, we came crashing down to earth. The Bantams put three past Steve Phillips and it was back to the drawing board for Davis and his leaky defence.

It's hard to explain, but that defeat at Valley Parade wasn't all bad. I travelled with a friend (from Leeds) and didn't sit with the Alex fans, so for once enjoyed a different perspective. The Bradford lads around me thought we looked okay, although I suppose you would say that when your team is romping home three nil. But there was belief amongst them that the Alex could win games, and that we would score goals. In Nick Powell, Ashley Westwood, AJ Leitch-Smith, Max Clayton and Luke Murphy (who all played a part that day) we had real talent and firepower in the side. We lost the match, heavily, but few could deny that life had been pumped into the team, and that certain individuals had already responded to the new coach. Davis just needed to harness the energy and enthusiasm to produce more consistent results. That was the crux of the matter: we required a prolonged unbeaten spell, and also needed to learn how to shut teams out.

The reverse in Yorkshire produced an immediate reaction at Bristol. In fact, that goal glut that Bantams fans predicted came days later as the New Year was welcomed with open arms. The Alex put five past Bristol Rovers as revellers got ready to paint the town red. And it wasn't a flash in the pan. Across the next seven games that took us from January to mid-February, the Alex won five. We sat in the top half of the table with forty one points on the board. The initial target of securing League Two safety was in touching distance and most of us had banished all fears of relegation. It was a very decent start.

So what did Davis bring to the table? As a youngster, he came to Crewe in the months after Stoke City released him. That teenager, then just 18 years old, was understandably gutted. Within a month, however, an unexpected call gave him a lifeline, a trial at the Alex under a new manager called Dario Gradi. Like the rest of us back in 1983, Davis had never heard of the fella. Still, when your future playing career depends on it I reckon you'd take a punt on most clubs. That the Alex was just down the A500 helped; so after impressing the gaffer he made his league debut away at Rochdale when Gradi himself was unveiled to fans at the start of the new season. He was a huge success, captaining the side within twelve months and winning several "Player of the Season" awards in his four years at the club. He was a winner. That positive mentality would play a big part in his early months as Crewe manager. As early as January 2012, he told reporters that he didn't 'like to talk about avoiding relegation' because it sounded negative. Getting to the 50-point safety mark was the priority, but that he wanted to 'really push on' as soon as possible. The ambitious young player was still hungry as he entered Football League management.

So there's a wonderful symmetry about the relationship, Davis coming back to Crewe to assume his first fully professional managerial role, once again under the watchful eye of his long-time mentor. It's stretching the old parable somewhat, but there's an element of the Prodigal Son about it. I just like the phrase. He was home, we had begun a fresh chapter, but nothing could prepare us for what the future held.

EIGHTEEN GAMES!

Valentine's Day 2012 brought more than red roses and chocolates for Alex fans. Wives and partners of long-suffering supporters heaved sighs of relief at 10pm that Tuesday night, as loved ones arrived home from the match against Burton with a spring in their step. Davis watched his side secure another three points in a game they controlled from start to finish. Even a 90th minute consolation goal by former Alex striker Calvin Zola didn't take the shine off a fabulous evening. The resurgence was going to plan.

Later that week, however, away at Southend, the Crewe manager was left scratching his head. His tactics didn't produce at least a point that many had craved leading up to the fixture. Despite fielding a strong side with significant firepower (including on-loan Greg Pearson, from Burton), the Alex lost 1-0 to a late strike. Davis bemoaned his side's missed opportunities but was content that his players had frustrated and tested one of the division's frontrunners. It was no disgrace, but recording his fourth defeat since taking over did not please the man unaccustomed to losing games. He worked the players hard across the next few days and produced a line-up ready to bounce back on the Tuesday night. Accrington Stanley were the victims.

The games were coming thick and fast and a number of supporters had noted that the team looked noticeably fitter under Davis' watch. Subtle changes were made week-to-week, and unlike his predecessor he used his substitutes freely. There were also regular tactical changes evident, and following a below-par first half against Stanley, the Crewe gaffer went for the jugular. Screams for a penalty when Nick Powell was felled went unheard, but the fast-improving Luke Murphy and rock-solid Ashley Westwood eventually gained a stranglehold on a scrappy game. From a corner earned by the home-grown midfield duo, it was super-sub Max Clayton who snatched the lead. Powell couldn't keep out of the referee's notebook (accused of diving when it should have been a spot-kick), but the visitors couldn't keep him off the score sheet either. He wrapped up the points in stoppage time to convince the home fans that, under Davis, the Alex could go the distance. It was mid-February, the Alex sat tenth in League Two and a solid unbeaten sequence had just begun.

After so long under the cosh, it was never likely to be straightforward. Supporters still needed to be convinced. That was the case after the next home game. Despite an exciting 3-3 draw with

Wimbledon, and another point, you'd have thought that Crewe had plunged into the relegation zone. The first "We Are Going Up" chants had started in the Gresty Road end, and a healthy crowd of 4,240 was preparing to go home happy.

BANG, BANG!

Two quick strikes for the Dons! I suppose the reaction was inevitable. Boos reverberated around Gresty Road as the visiting players celebrated an unlikely comeback. Sloppy football never goes down well. The Southend defeat aside, the home support had developed an appetite for winning. Davis was livid; not with the fickle fans who were shell-shocked after watching their side concede twice in nine minutes, but with his players who had thrown away two precious points when the game should have been wrapped up. Needlessly chucking away points was infuriating. Davis gave the players both barrels, and he pulled no punches when speaking to reporters: 'I don't want people here who are going to capitulate under pressure. I want them to become men and push the club forward.' As fans we love such tough words, knowing that anything less than 100% will not be tolerated. Like the more exacting fitness regime and increased use of substitutes, it was a refreshing sea change.

For nearly a decade I have become accustomed to watching schoolboy football as my two lads have progressed up the age groups. The games have become increasingly skilful, faster and more competitive. From the sidelines it's been fascinating studying the other parents. I like to shout and encourage, but I vowed from the start that I'd never get carried away. I always wanted the boys to enjoy playing. On a more professional footing that has always been the ethos at Crewe, certainly since Gradi developed the academy system. His footballers were praised, allowed to express themselves, and there was less emphasis on results. That is fine with juniors, but there must come a point when a more ruthless, winning mentality is instilled.

That's what Davis brought to the table. He didn't want to witness schoolboy errors at Gresty Road, and he seemed to know that the fans demanded better. Wimbledon played an open, attacking style that day, and the Alex could and should have thrashed them. We even missed a penalty. Post-match the gaffer elaborated: 'I am still in shock, I really can't believe it. I've spoken to the lads about it. They were terrific in the first half. The movement, the passing, the chances were created - it should have been five or six,' he told *The Crewe Chronicle*. '(At half time) we talked about complacency, dropping back, inviting pressure - and then we went and did it. We did all those things. They are obviously not listening, or they can't do it. It has hurt me. I hope it has hurt the players,' he added.

The verbal storm passed and his tough stance paid dividends. The defence tightened up, and across the next three games there was a new-found cohesion evident throughout the squad. What delighted me was watching the players respond so quickly, especially as the pressure mounted. Rearranged fixtures meant that a four-week period brought relentless Tuesday/Saturday fixtures. The fringe players were vital, and they had to slot in seamlessly and uphold the work ethic, urgency and desire the boss demanded.

Against Port Vale, there was a midweek trip to Burslem that offered Crewe fans, and Davis, the opportunity to improve upon the point earned at Gresty Road earlier in the season. Byron Moore scored that day and he scored again at Vale Park. It was a late equaliser but fully deserved. An unchanged side from the previous game took heed of the manager's words and limited the home side to a handful of chances. There were hairy moments, clear-cut opportunities to penetrate the Alex defence. But the team stood firm, and we ventured forward quickly when we regained possession. It wasn't a smash-and-grab mission; far from it. The Alex players were disciplined, and only an unlucky deflection off Dave Artell had given Vale the lead. Crewe fought back and showed the spirit and heart that Davis wanted from anyone who pulled on the red shirt. Moore levelled with ten minutes remaining. The camaraderie was infectious. The fans lapped it up. Lee Bell was even cautioned, despite being a substitute on the sidelines! The Alex manager smirked; he was in tune with the fans. It was an unnecessary booking but worth the yellow card, as it brought supporters, players and management together. The siege mentality was developing fast. We hadn't seen that before at Crewe.

***

So what was the catalyst and what clicked to bring about such accord? A few key relationships blossomed, player-manager bonds that would unify the team and facilitate one of the most remarkable turnarounds witnessed at Gresty Road. Davis and Baker were obviously instrumental, pulling together numerous factions and getting the best from previously under-performing or stalled players. But one young man stands out for me; and he was head and shoulders above of the rest. Nick Powell: the broody teenager who would not look out of place alongside Robert Pattinson in the *Twilight Saga* box office smash. But let's forget his flop of hair and pallid complexion; instead, we should concentrate on the quick feet, vision, creativity and outstanding football brain.

First, we must wind back to the previous August to an incident that would prove decisive in his development. The Alex lost 2-0 away to Shrewsbury. It was the team's fifth straight defeat. Gradi was struggling to get anything from his players, let alone Powell. The temperamental playmaker saw red - quite literally. Sent off on 68 minutes, just eight minutes after he came on as a substitute, he left the Alex floundering when the game was still in the balance at 1-0. The extra man was enough, and the home side delivered the killer blow deep into injury time.

Powell needed to be carefully managed. In theory Gradi was the perfect teacher. But with headstrong lads bursting onto the scene, I wonder if this was the generation that cracked the maestro and convinced him to concentrate on the age groups below the first team? Gradi mostly played Powell as a substitute in his debut season; when he was a sixteen-year-old. Few break into the senior side that early, but he was ready. Of slight build, his pace, natural athleticism and youthful strength was enough to give him a chance alongside wisened pros. But Gradi decided to err on the side of caution, as he often did with emerging talent. His job always was to temper the exuberance, that lust to create, dazzle and play-make when good old-fashioned discipline was needed out on the pitch. Timing was everything to the man. It frustrated us, and for years supporters scratched their heads as players described as "the next big thing" faded from the squad. They were often sent out on loan to clubs two or three levels below us. Seeing players reach nineteen, twenty and twenty-one without establishing themselves was always likely to dishearten the watching public. At Crewe, persevering with such players seemed madness as it stretched an already meagre budget. With Powell, having identified the undoubted potential, there was little chance he was going to be held back or sent out on loan.

Across the 2010/11 season the kid was introduced nineteen times, more often than not around the 85th minute mark. That was too late to make a real difference, and certainly too late for a young man with an unquenchable thirst to play the game. For once, the steady, slowly-but-surely approach was probably not the right route to regular first-team action.

In his second season, Powell was again frustrated by Gradi. In the months before Davis took control, he played thirteen games and scored just once. He started more games but the goals eluded him. He was still finding his feet, but perhaps the "Gradi way" was to hold back, restrict the player and use him in a more rigid team structure. And how many times over the years did we hear Gradi chastise players for shooting at goal when a pass was the better option? Powell needed to roam, to be the focal point for Alex attacks. Walking the ball into the net was not his style, although he would do that later to prove that he could score in any way he chose. Those around him needed to sign up, support him, distract defenders and accept that he would be the centre of attention. For that to happen in any team you must deliver. So with Gradi in charge we didn't see the best of the youngster.

However, following the red card so early in the 2011/12 campaign, it was obvious that Powell needed reining in. What Gradi did was change the young player's mind set. There was a psychological realignment, a tweak, and a gentle nod in the right direction. The world was not out to get him, just a few robust and uncompromising defenders tasked with halting his flow. He had to deal with that. If he didn't, or if the Alex coaches could not assist and develop that side of his game, well, he could have faded. What a waste that would have been!

Thankfully, Powell emerged from Gradi-spun cotton wool raring to go. When Davis picked up the baton in the autumn he had one of the best prospects outside the Championship at his disposal. Tall and imposing, although he was yet to fill out, Powell offered pace, determination, vision, outrageous skill and, crucially, goals. He started to score freely. With the dismissal put behind him, many felt that he returned to the fold with a fresh outlook. He was any manager's dream, if he could be effectively integrated to play as part of a team. So Davis inherited a side in the wrong half of League Two but boasting a few gems that, with a little polish, could sparkle and set the Alex apart from the rest.

Davis gave the likes of Powell, Clayton and Murphy freedom, and from the outset I think that the new gaffer wanted to promote the club's home-grown talent to a greater extent than his mentor, especially the crop of 2009/10 that he'd seen when Thordarson brought him to the club.

More so than the other graduates, when he was in the right frame of mind Powell was capable of anything. Davis watched and helped to develop him each day at Reaseheath. He appreciated what the player had to offer, and perhaps formulated plans to harness Powell's skills ahead of his ascension to the Alex throne. By his own admission, Davis struggled to understand the lad initially. He was a complex individual who had all the traits of a genius footballer. With such prodigious talent often comes baggage - a single-mindedness that does not sit comfortably with the team ethic. The Alex, however, needed a talisman, someone to excite and stir the emotions amongst supporters, but also one that would rise above the division's mediocrity and win points.

***

Back to that winning sequence that was slowly gaining momentum. Coincidentally, it was Shrewsbury lining up at Gresty Road. This time, there were no red cards. Powell had matured. He was in the right place at the right time. There was nothing flash about the finish. His deft touch from a Westwood free-kick secured a point and took his tally for the season to nine (all competitions). But there was no showboating. As the game progressed he kept the ball sensibly. The outrageous passes, long-range shots and audacious flicks and nutmegs were put on hold as the clock wound down. The Alex probed and looked for a winner but there was no recklessness - especially not from Powell. At one point he hugged the touchline, turned, beat two defenders, looped back to the corner flag and dazzled the home crowd like a matador as he retained possession to the disgust of several Shrewsbury bulls. They knew that they had no chance of liberating the ball without the use of foul play. Even cynical kicks to the shin and calf failed to enrage him. He defended from the front. Davis, Baker and the fans applauded him as he left the pitch. He had learnt his lesson; the Shrew hadn't been tamed, but it was no longer so wild.

By now the main stand was awash with men making notes, scouts from myriad clubs keen to check out what Crewe Alexandra had to offer. One name was underlined and marked with fancy highlighters every week. Powell was far too good for League Two, even at this embryonic stage of his career. Any spotter would have singled out the midfield attacker as one to watch, one to nobble even. I wouldn't say that he was the fulcrum of the side - just yet - as Westwood, Moore and Murphy were equally prominent and potent. But while they blocked, controlled and passed to help dominate games, they were not returning the same number of goals, that precious commodity that every club covets.

Davis knew what he had in his armour; a lethal attacker that frightened every opposing team. Powell's confidence flowed through the side and others rode the wave of positivity. Otherwise average players broke free and also showed what they had to offer. It was still hard for the fan base to comprehend, but the team was now on the charge. The stars were aligning. The games could not come fast enough.

Rotherham got lucky; not with the point in a 1-1 draw at their temporary Don Valley Stadium, but because Crewe were without Powell and Clayton; both away on England U18 duty. Still, it was another solid result. The progress wasn't rampant, but the Alex remained unbeaten for a fifth consecutive match. That was the best sequence in over a year.

Away at Gillingham, however, Powell was at it again. And what a contribution he made; a quite spectacular wallop from thirty five yards out started the scoring. Of course it wasn't an uncontrolled "boot" from a player hopeful that he might hit the target. He knew exactly what he was doing. The goalkeeper shuffled, leapt and flapped for the cameras, but he had no chance when the ball left Powell's foot. It was a missile, locked on to its target. And when the home side thought they were back in the game Powell hit them hard again.

First he set up AJ Leitch-Smith with a perfectly-weighted pass, then he claimed a third with a classy left-foot shot. An increasingly frustrated Gillingham stopper balked at his defenders, but against the rampant Alex front men they were left stranded. Powell was everywhere. He should have taken the matchball home, but was denied twice. Those misses, and a wasted opportunity from Moore, looked to have cost Crewe all three points. Two lapses in concentration let Gillingham back into the game. It was fabulous entertainment, poised at 3-3, with both sides looking to attack at every opportunity.

Into the final minutes and there was no let-up, especially from Crewe. The referee had already checked his watch, the crowd was starting to whistle and some of the home fans were filtering out of the exits. Gills gaffer Andy Hessenthaler was going berserk on the touchline. His side deserved a draw and he didn't want to throw a point away in the dying seconds. They'd fought hard, delivered some exciting football and done enough to win the match themselves. But time was up. Avoiding defeat was now the priority. The Alex had other ideas; and to show that Davis had turned things around the team needed to win games. So it was fitting that super-sub Clayton hit the fourth - the winner; a cheeky glancing header.

FOUR-THREE TO THE RAILWAYMEN!

The jubilation verged on hysteria. Seconds later the whistle sounded and everyone went berserk. All four goals were scored by home-grown players. It was a stunning result. The Gills had won four straight games prior to Crewe's visit. Their fans left the ground in shock while Alex supporters' madcap celebrations continued. The more optimistic even started a chorus of "We Are Going Up..." to rub further salt into Gillingham's wounds. Also evident was the desire of the Alex management to engage with those who backed the club each week. It was easy at Gresty Road, a quick wave to the main stand usually sufficient. But on the road, making the effort to walk over to the travellers meant a lot - to all concerned. The players joined Davis and Baker and applauded the vocal efforts of four hundred that afternoon. It was bonding on a massive scale.

The question asked on the train home was whether the Alex had any chance of contesting a play-off place. Winning so dramatically in Kent added fuel to the fire, but it was still a ludicrous notion. Months earlier we'd talked about relegation, even losing our league status. Suddenly everyone was positive, excited about matchday, wondering how many goals we'd score, whether Powell would deliver another "worldy" strike, and if we'd keep a clean sheet. It was all crazy dialogue, upbeat chatter that we hadn't enjoyed over pints for five or six years. I was unstoppable. At one point I was seriously eyeing up top spot, meticulously calculating the points for umpteen scenarios that could take us close to the division's frontrunners. Madness!

Two further back-to-back wins really set Alex hearts racing and left me thinking that Davis was going to take us up as champions. Much of the hype revolved around Powell, and at this point I need to temper my enthusiasm for him. Each week I acted like a love-struck teenager. That sounds so wrong, but I hadn't harboured such "football" feelings since Dean Ashton roused similar passions nearly a decade earlier. It's something that only very special players can awaken. When they announce themselves it's a joy attending matches. Each week you know something extraordinary will happen: a sublime pass, crazy piece of control or ridiculously extravagant goal. Powell was that man, just as Ashton, Danny Murphy and David Platt were before him.

Thankfully, I did not have his poster on my bedroom door, nor did I have his name on the back of my replica shirt. But I spoke about him endlessly. It was an obsession, no doubt about that. Had I been a few years younger I would have chased him down the street begging for an autograph. Thankfully, the old knees ensured that I retained my dignity.

As an aside, around this time I had another writing project in mind. I'd covered a number of angles over the years but I had always fancied tracking one of the club's up-and-coming players from academy through to the first team, and then beyond if and when a move to the Championship or Premier League became a reality. With a little luck there would be international appearances along the way. So Powell was the perfect fit.

He was already halfway there. Through a friend who had coached the lad at junior school I made contact; and yes, I was star struck. I held it together and swapped a few notes, outlining what I hoped to achieve with the project. He didn't dismiss the idea initially but he boxed clever. Max Clayton was, he told me, the better option. He liked doing the media stuff, whereas Powell didn't. Besides, posting his thoughts on Twitter had already earned him a ticking off with the club. So he didn't want to get himself into trouble again. He wanted to keep a low profile.

But I had my heart set on a story involving Powell. He was the next major export, I was convinced about that. He fell short on so many fronts, but at seventeen years of age he was the stand-out Alex player. Clayton had the pace, the touch and a nose for goal, but there was something about Powell that set him apart. He was special, and I suspect that he knew it. I also believe that he was shy, almost withdrawn, and most definitely a very complex character. He was a superstar in the making. His final word on the book idea was a resounding "NO". Bugger!

Against Swindon he was sublime. His volley mid-way through the first half almost broke the crossbar. The ball clipped the underside, bounced down and nestled satisfyingly in the back of the net. There was no goal-line controversy. The Robins' goalkeeper sat there, bemused, wondering what had just flown past him at pace. Powell was already acknowledging the applause as his team mates chased him to the corner flag. Visiting manager Paulo Di Canio was speechless. The scouts scribbled notes furiously, as they would several times across the ninety minutes as the wonder kid threatened more goals.

The Alex were beating the league leaders, and with a team of home-grown kids comfortably outwitting some big names that had cost serious money.

CAN WE PLAY YOU EVERY WEEK?

We taunted the Wiltshire fans on the Popside with menace and delight. They had no response. Like their manager, they were shell-shocked. And it got worse for them. Westwood sealed the points, but Dave Artell and Adam Dugdale deserved much credit. They kept the Swindon frontmen under wraps. Containing a side that had already scored 61 league goals was no mean feat. Matt Tootle gave his usual 100% and Steve Phillips made dramatic late saves with his legs when the visitors finally showed the form that had taken them to the top of the division. They were not good enough against Crewe, and any neutrals watching would have assumed that the Alex were first and not eighth in the table.

The relentless fixture pile-up continued on the Tuesday night when Bradford came to town. They also went home disappointed, pointless and without a goal to their name. Harry Davis kept a cool head to convert yet again from the penalty spot, and his calm finish proved to be enough. The Alex players limped over the finishing line that evening, and it was another case of the result carrying more importance than the performance. But when you are winning games, there is always a little extra in the tank, and despite a ten-minute barrage, the Bantams could not break us down. At last we could defend a lead. The roar that greeted the final whistle was both elation and relief. The unbeaten run continued, and although it was taking its toll it was worth it.

EIGHT GAMES UNBEATEN!

Even then, over two months since our last defeat, promotion was still unthinkable, and yet with momentum building that delicious "P" word was on everyone's lips. A constant pre-match talking point around the pubs was the incomprehensible transformation across three or four short months. It was wonderful, and turning up on matchday became a pleasure, something every Alex supporter looked forward to across the working week.

The short timespan also made it harder to deal with. As fans, we had endured five seasons of decline, inevitably slipping from the Championship, but then struggling in League One and finally imploding when our return to the basement was sealed away at Edgeley Park in April 2009. So the newfound swagger was difficult to accept at first. It was a phase, a short blip that would soon fizzle out. There was a reluctance to get sucked in, fooled into believing that everything was alright. It was all too good to be true.

The players had no such concerns and there was no let-up away at Hereford; the Alex nudged ever closer to a play-off spot with a close-fought 1-0 win at the quaint old Edgar Street ground. By now the supporters were knackered, so the players must have been feeling the pressure - both physically and emotionally. But they had adrenaline on their side, and when Murphy snatched the winner eleven minutes from time it was no problem finding the energy to celebrate his goal in style. It wasn't elegant that afternoon, and Hereford created the better chances. But Crewe had players that could light up a scrappy encounter with flashes of brilliance. And in Davis they now had a manager prepared to take risks. He threw Clayton into the action when others would have shored up the defence and played for a point. The fresh legs unsettled the hosts, and it was a neat move between Clayton and Moore that lead to Murphy's goal. The travelling Alex fans rose as one to salute another fabulous three points. It was now about winning, and regularly.

There are countless players worth a mention at this point, and for once I will avoid heaping any more praise on young Powell. Instead, at the other end of the field, old pros Dave Artell and goalkeeper Steve Phillips were outstanding. Week after week they contained players nearly half their age, but used every ounce of experience to their advantage. Adam Dugdale was a titan, prepared to battle for every ball. Harry Davis was assured, calculated with his distribution and sound in the air. Matt Tootle and Kelvin Mellor were another two academy boys showing immense potential, both confident and comfortable on the ball. Danny Shelley was versatile and offered a superb buffer between the back four and midfield. And the engine room purred with Westwood, Murphy and Bell on song. Possession was already a key factor, and Crewe dominated most games. Even the corner count was favourable, something else that improved under Davis. Up front Moore, Leitch-Smith and Clayton all provided options and they could all sniff out a goal. By now the regular/settled team picked from the core matchday squad of sixteen was, on its day, a match for any club in the division.

Looking back it is still hard trying to explain the confidence that oozed as each matchday dawned. Losing was not on the agenda, the word almost blanked from Alex fans' vocabularies by this stage. Some were arrogant, no doubt about that, but it was warranted. Pete Morse from the local *Chronicle* summed it up, writing that Davis had 'instilled a winning habit which could take Crewe all the way to Wembley' if the unbeaten run continued as we all expected.

And it did persist deep into April, although the juggernaut was forced to apply the brakes a little. At home to Northampton there was a whiff of disappointment when the game ended 1-1, and then away at Crawley the following Good Friday afternoon the scoreline was the same. The Alex hit the bar, missed a penalty and created the better opportunities in both games, but had to settle for two points from a potential six. Davis and the players had set themselves a high standard, so it was no surprise learning that the dressing room had been quiet after both matches. The manager had to cajole them, emphasise what they had already achieved and prepare them for the next challenge.

Whatever Davis said at Crawley carried through to Easter Monday when Bristol Rovers travelled up from the West Country. They would later wish that their coach had broken down, as the Alex battered them.

Crewe attacked at will, won a deserved penalty and should have had two more. Rovers kicked and hacked, anything to stop the flow. There was even a rare goal for defender Kelvin Mellor such was the home side's dominance across the 3-0 win. At one point I wondered if Steve Phillips was going to leave his goalmouth when the Alex won a corner. But this victory was also disciplined and well planned. Every player knew his job, occasional errors were corrected by team mates offering cover and even the overly physical challenges by desperate Bristol players were met with an Alex wall of players quick to leap forward to defend their colleagues. This was the game that convinced me that Crewe Alexandra were heading for the end-of-season play-offs. It was just a case of where we'd finish the season, and whether we'd gain home advantage in the second leg of the semi-final. Everyone was now that confident.

The most incredible post-match reaction came under the main stand after the referee had put Rovers out of their misery. Having wrestled my way to the bar, lager finally in hand, I took a few seconds to admire the league table that was flashed on the screens around the room. We were poised to make our final surge into the top seven, just goal difference now pegging us back in eighth position. Stood in front of me, muttering into his beer, an old fella looked to his mate and suggested that we'd blown it in late February and early March. He was serious, so I couldn't stop myself questioning his logic. Drawing four back-to-back games (Wimbledon, Vale, Shrewsbury and Rotherham) had, he maintained, ruined any chance of automatic promotion. It was an almighty effort, but I resisted the urge to pour my pint over his head. He wasn't worth three quid and I walked away to relay the tale to the lads. It was ridiculous; still only four months after many had worryingly assessed the "wrong" end of the division each Saturday evening, here was a man effectively accusing Davis and the team of failure. Now I am fully aware that you can never please all of the people all of the time, but come on! The old codger should have been arrested, locked in a dark room and shipped out to Vale Park every other week.

The next two weeks were a blur. I couldn't concentrate at work, on day-to-day tasks or family stuff; instead I checked the league table and tried to calculate how many points we needed from the next four games. We got one on the Saturday, but that miserable bloke from the main stand bar would have muttered "told you so" when Macclesfield held us 2-2 at Moss Rose. Former Alex midfielder Colin Daniel equalised ten minutes from time, and some wondered if the Alex wheels were coming off.

Now we were sweating. It was tight, although seventh place was still up for grabs. Davis didn't falter though. He rolled out more optimistic sound bites and continued to emphasise the positives. It worked again, as the Alex beat Cheltenham 1-0 at home. Now it was in our hands.

FOURTEEN GAMES UNBEATEN!

The most outstanding statistic to emerge from that slender but deserved win was that Dave Artell grabbed the only goal of the match. There's nothing too unusual about the big fella getting on the score sheet, with a thundering header more often than not. But Artell's goal that mid-April afternoon was the first by a non-academy product since on-loan Greg Pearson scored against Wimbledon back in February. Eleven consecutive games boasted home-grown goalscorers. They are all worth a mention: Powell, naturally, claimed six; Harry Davis smashed three (all penalties); Moore and Leitch-Smith chipped in with two each; Murphy also grabbed a couple; while Clayton, Westwood and Mellor scored one. It was incredible, and I double-checked the statistics to convince myself that I wasn't penning wishful thoughts!

Without checking details further afield, I very much doubt that any other professional club could boast similar. And of the players making up the side, only Phillips, Artell and Billy Bodin (on loan from Swindon) had started regular games during February-April, which denied Davis fielding eleven lads developed on the Reaseheath pitches. It reaffirmed the club's commitment to youth. Unlike Steve Holland and Gudjon Thordarson before him, Davis hadn't looked far beyond the club's academy to fill his matchday squad. Against Cheltenham, for example, of the 16 men listed, eleven had learned their trade under the watchful eyes of the Crewe coaches. Every one of them played a part in the match, three coming on as a substitute. Perhaps it was the timing, with the academy now burgeoning and the club playing League Two football but, more so than even Gradi had ever done, the new manager was "going with our own" like never before.

The play-off spot drew ever closer down in Devon. On paper 1-1 against Torquay didn't look too spectacular, but YET ANOTHER outrageous contribution from Powell did the business. Crewe pressed, the ball zipped across the Torquay area, Powell held his position on the edge of the box, and when the opportunity presented itself he took it. The ball flew into the bottom corner past helpless defenders and a dismayed goalkeeper. In fact, that 90th minute leveller kept the momentum going and convinced us that Davis' young guns were the real deal. It was a game that we would probably have lost under Gradi's tenure. With the

Davis-Baker combo in full flow, there was no letting up until the referee had left the pitch. At Plainmoor around 800 went crazy as other results left us sitting comfortably in that oh-so sweet play-off zone.

FIFTEEN GAMES UNBEATEN!

For the record, the final game also ended all square. A 2-2 draw at home to Aldershot was another fair result. Crucially, it secured the play-off position. But the visitors caused panic when they grabbed the lead on the stroke of half time and Alex fans checked to see how Oxford were doing. They were losing against Port Vale. As the players left the field, matchday announcer Andy Scoffin said "That's not in the script" as he walked out to chat with fans and mascots. He was right. We had all hoped for a less complicated conclusion to the season.

Thankfully, Murphy scored the goal that made us certainties for the play-off places. So Davis watched his side recover from 2-1 down. It proved yet again that we now had added steel. There was abundant flair, determination and goals throughout the team. It was not the gung-ho end-of-season romp many hoped for, but the unbeaten run was intact. That was enough. It was all about the route to Wembley now. There were no serious injuries (just Dave Artell recovering) or suspensions looming; this was a remarkable time to be an Alex fan.

***

The two draws to wrap up the standard season of forty-six games was an appropriate finish. Davis was still rebuilding, coaxing and teasing the best from his players. Racing into the automatic promotion places would have left us off guard, with everyone assuming that all performance issues had been ironed out. They had not. There were still cracks in the armour. We had not become the Arsenal "invincibles" overnight, despite what many thought. The play-off route was perfect, as it left the Alex manager with work to do but also gave everyone added excitement going into May. We needed that, desperately. It had been a dire few years. This was our tonic.

One mildly interesting statistic was that we finished eleven points shy of fourth-placed Southend; they were our opponents in the two-leg semi-final that would take place the following week. The Shrimpers had missed out on promotion by one point. They even had a superior goal difference to third-place Crawley. A scoreless draw at Torquay in mid-April proved to be their undoing in an otherwise faultless run-in. They were deflated, now forced to play on and against a team with great momentum.

Southend had edged both league games against Crewe during the season, winning 2-0 at Gresty Road and by a single goal at Roots Hall back in February. And of course that 1-0 defeat for Crewe kick-started the unbeaten sequence. We were a form side, but they had the best away record in the division. Southend had every right to go into the two-leg showdown brimming with confidence. They would expect to win and would be cocksure that they'd secure promotion via the play-off route.

The Internet forums suggested otherwise. Their fans became cautious. They knew what Crewe Alexandra had become post-Gradi. A few tried Steve "Interesting" Davis snooker-style gags, but they were feeble attempts to deflect attention from the serious football banter that started as we prepared for the encounter at Gresty Road. Psychologically, I reckon we had the advantage.

That match, our chance to establish a solid lead ahead of the Roots Hall return, took place on Saturday 12th May. A fabulous crowd of 7,221 reminiscent of the Championship days roared as the teams emerged from the tunnel. The air bristled with excitement and anticipation. Eleven Alex lions marched into the centre circle, chests puffed out, last-minute orders from Davis still ringing in their ears. They didn't need motivating by this point; this was game number seventeen in the crazy run. They wanted it to continue. Defeat wasn't an option. I called them "lions", but they looked more like cubs. Nine of the starting eleven were products of the Crewe academy, with goalkeeper Steve Phillips and defender Carl Martin completing the line-up. Only the Alex 'keeper had any play-off experience to his name. The home-grown kids had an average age of just over 21 years!

In the stands the considerably older supporters started to fret. That fearless aura from previous weeks evaporated as battle commenced. We looked down at mere mortals and wished they were gods. Southend looked a threat and brought with them the best away record in League Two. So there was a definite game plan deployed that afternoon. There had to be. Bilel Mohsni had smashed three past Crewe in the two league games, so he had to be stopped.

The answer was height and power at the back. With Dave Artell injured (a broken foot sustained in training) in came Carl Martin, and the diminutive Matt Tootle was nudged into midfield. That meant central defensive spots for Harry Davis and Adam Dugdale, with Kelvin Mellor at right-back. All four defenders tipped the scales at six feet and one inch. That proved crucial, as the dominant Alex rearguard kept the visiting strikers quiet in the first half and delivered a sucker punch immediately after the interval. Dugdale rose highest when he tucked inside Mohsni, his towering French marker, and met Westwood's cross perfectly.

GOAL!

A header, albeit well placed beyond the Southend goalkeeper, but what a moment of sheer exhilaration. Duggy went crazy, unaccustomed to scoring. The rest of the team mobbed him. They ran to the Alex fans and almost caused a riot. The season was alive and kicking, the chance of promotion soared and pound signs lit up the directors' eyes.

The goal brought huge relief but within seconds we were demanding more. One is never enough, especially when the stakes are so high. We needed a cushion. So the rest of the second half was torture, especially when Phillips was tested. He stood firm, as did the whole team. We held our breath; some covered their eyes. The Alex players were magnificent, defending from the front, holding the ball and sensibly keeping possession. Then Powell slipped a cheeky ball through to Leitch-Smith, and over 6,000 Crewe fans watched spellbound as the Crewe lad's lob was tipped inches over the bar. So close, but no second goal.

Powell, for once not on the scoresheet, impressed for other reasons. First, he kept his head, showed maturity in the face of persistent provocation and got on with his game. The Southend midfield and defence hacked and chopped at the teenager but failed to get a reaction. Second, he stuck to the script. Davis had a plan and Powell helped to implement it. They all did. It showed in their faces when the whistle sounded and the roof lifted. It was a job well done.

NEARLY THERE!

The question on every fan's lips was whether the single goal lead was going to be enough? Thankfully, the play-offs are stacked so that you have little time to worry. The second leg, down south, came four days later. The Alex manager was again bullish in his comments to the media as we got ready to do battle: 'We will put our heads where it hurts, get blocks in, put our bodies on the line and we will do it together' he said. That never-say-die attitude was epitomised by the rock that is Dave Artell. Despite sporting a broken bone in his foot he declared himself fit to play. And he was needed, as Southend came at Crewe like a train from the start.

It was a ding-dong encounter. A clever first-half strike from Leitch-Smith was cancelled out midway through the second period by the vastly experienced Neil Harris. Southend had already blasted against the post - twice! Then the effervescent Clayton popped up in the 86th minute with what everyone believed was the winner, a cute finish under pressure. There was a two-goal cushion. We were cruising, Wembley tickets as good as booked. The party started early in the Crewe end, but crashed to a halt when Southend's Chris Barker headed the equaliser two minutes later.

Then it was carnage. Every mistake, attack or free-kick caused panic. We had to hold on, but Southend found an extra gear. The home fans pushed them on, demanding one more assault on the Alex goal. But it didn't happen.

The draw was hard-earned, in fact much more than that. It was an epic performance. We attacked, tried to play football, and then defended as though our lives depended upon it. Three Alex players entered the referee's notebook (Davis, Leitch-Smith and Powell), proving beyond doubt that they were prepared to mix it up as well as play an attractive passing game.

EIGHTEEN GAMES!

They did it the hard way, and survived a few scares but there were scenes of ecstasy as the players celebrated with fans at the final whistle. Dugdale's goal in the first leg was the difference. Over 180 minutes we emerged victorious; 3-2 the aggregate score. It was magical, at least for us. The Alex management were on their knees looking to the heavens. Then they hugged, punched the air, and conducted the crowd in raucous song. They grabbed scarves and flags from supporters, waving them wildly because they were also fans that night. They'd done it; we'd done it. Brilliant!

Elsewhere there were footballers in tears. Shrimpers boss Paul Sturrock stopped short of falling to the ground, but his body language yelled pain. His side came so close but, ultimately, failed at the final hurdle. Their supporters walked away, heads bowed. It was a wasted season to them.

As Davis and Bakes finally stopped cavorting about on the pitch, there was a smug satisfaction on many faces. It was a small detail, but one that matters to football supporters. Southend went into the two-legged tie thinking they'd turn us over. They were the last team to beat the Alex, way back in mid-February. They had been cocky. They wrote us off as hopeful pretenders. So it was immensely satisfying to deny them a trip to the final.

Petty-minded grudges aside, the Alex were now in the play-off final. Davis had done it. In less than six months he'd turned things around, stopped the rot, and instilled confidence in a ravaged squad. Most importantly, he had given the supporters hope. That had been in short supply. Now the dreaming was over, and a trip to "new" Wembley was about to become reality. Eighteen games unbeaten; the most important "nineteenth" was still to come.

THE GREEN MAN

For several years I'd put off a sneaky visit to the revamped home of English football. Old Wembley back in '97 was my last day in the North London sunshine. Along with circa 13,000 Alex fans, we broke Brentford hearts that day. It was a special occasion, a real "Sunday Best" experience. So when the gleaming new structure rose up, complete with dazzling arch, there was a yearning to return; but not at any cost, for any old game. In the back of my mind I was always conscious that it would be cheating, going along to a Johnstone's Paint Trophy final, a half-full international friendly or even the non-league FA Vase showcase. Getting tickets for any of those would have been relatively simple, and yet it would not have involved the Alex. Being unfaithful was not an option. So I'd been saving myself, all virginal for the extravaganza laid on by Steve Davis after that implausible dash for the play-offs.

The build-up started immediately after Southend heads dropped. We would face Cheltenham, and promotion fever swept the town of Crewe. There was the customary rush for tickets, absolutely bonkers as the Alex would never sell out their allocation of seats. And yet we queued, the Englishness getting the better of us. The reward was Spaceship Wembley, an utterly fabulous far-off place, especially for the smaller clubs. It is a rare treat, where only the Premier League clubs usually hang out. It's also enormous. Unless you are one of the fallen giants, it is usual to see swathes of empty seats no matter how the cunning stadium administrators dish out the blocks of tickets. The TV cameras also do their best to make it look full, but more often than not the League Two final plays out to a backdrop of emptiness.

Such details don't matter to your obsessive fan. Those tickets are like gold dust, Willy Wonka specials. We simply had to have them - and on the day they go on sale. So I queued up with Ray, part of a snaking line that extended from the ticket office, round past the club shop, down the main stand and beyond the glass facade of the offices. I suppose four hundred stood wearily in front of us, all with shopping lists for mates, colleagues from work, neighbours and long-lost cousins who had not set foot in the town for years. Some needed two; others wanted twenty. But it was the play-off final, nobody cared that it was going to take hours. We'd come armed with stiff upper lips.

It helped that it was a decent day. The sun popped in and out, players appeared to boost morale, and the local reporters descended with notepads and cameras looking for the essential pre-Wembley quotes and pictures to fill the latest editions. Everyone obliged, holding scarves, banners and wearing jesters' hats, and then rolling out clichés on demand about it being "All Change" for Crewe, and "Full Steam Ahead" up the leagues.

The daft thing is, no matter how old you are getting those shiny tickets in your hand makes you feel like a kid at Christmas. You have something that thousands do not. The seat number is special, not just one of ninety-odd thousand. You are part of something. It is a sobering moment. Suddenly it's all very real. Crewe Alexandra vs Cheltenham Town; the date, the time, the venue… it was all there in beautiful shimmering letters. Images of fans and the trophy leap out from the quality paper complete with mesmerising hologram security patch. It was utterly magical.

WEMBLEY, WEMBLEY!

And before you ask, of course I didn't sleep the night before the match. Multiple messages had flown between the lads; what time we were travelling, where to meet, whether to take snacks and what top to wear. Don't laugh, but there was considerable deliberation selecting the right colour and vintage replica shirt. In the end, I opted for classy 1993/94 Vandanel White. Perfect for a sweltering day and a throw-back to happier times when Neil Lennon, Ashley Ward and Robbie Savage ruled the roost. All of the above had been checked, double-checked, folded and tucked away safely. And don't ask how many times I looked at the match tickets that had been carefully stashed in the kitchen drawer!

Yes, that's tickets plural. It was a monumental fixture, a defining moment in the club's history, so I had made a dramatic decision: I was taking the wife and kids. Now as readers of "*She Wore A Scarlet Ribbon*" will know, Mrs H stopped attending games a long time ago. It was never her thing, and to be honest she cramped my style. It always was a day out with the lads I had known for years. My two sons, well, the ungrateful gits cast aside childhood memories of sitting behind the Gresty Road end goal, exotic trips to Burnley, Wigan and Stoke, then threw it all in my face by deciding to support Chelsea when they were at primary school. Good luck to them getting tickets for Stamford Bridge. And yet I couldn't exclude them. This was Crewe, their birth town, and there's always the glimmer of hope that as teenage boys they might have a rethink. So instead of the booze cruise, the fast train or even a London stop-over with old mates, we booked onto one of the early-morning "official" coaches. That, as any parent knows, adds to the logistical nightmare. I could survive without drinks, mints, tissues and a sick bag no worries;

but the kids and mother-hen wife, oh no. You had to prepare for every eventuality. At one point a small travel suitcase was mentioned. I just made sure that my old fisherman's hat was ready; the forecast was Scorchio!

The alarm clock sounded at 5am; I could finally get up. The unwritten rule states quite clearly that I, the man of the house, must wake the kids and wife. That is easier said than done. I was chomping at the bit, ready to walk down the M6 and M1 motorways if necessary, but the non-partisan trio were still snoring. Even the waft of bacon butties up the stairs fell short of the mark, so it was duvets whipped off beds to finally rouse them. I was in no mood to hang around. It was matchday, the most significant matchday in years; I was already grumpy.

We made the coach with time to spare and thankfully bagged one of the early departures. It was chaos outside the Alex. Random coaches rolled up, and groups of two, five, ten and twenty all scrambled to get on first. It could and should have been much better organised. But when you are already intoxicated with crazy pre-match dreams, such trivial travel chaos is quickly forgotten. We got on, and luckily stayed together as a handy block of four. When the convoy headed south there were rumours that one coach had failed to turn up. Frustrated supporters were pacing furiously waiting for a replacement, burning shoe leather and chewing finger nails to stumps. I was just happy that I hadn't lost the kids.

The trouble with coach travel is the lengthy list of rules, regulations and annoying quirks. There's no beer allowed to settle your nerves, someone always rams their knees into the back of your seat, the on-board toilet is used by someone to dispose of a curry from the night before, the driver needs multiple fag breaks, and when you do stop off at the services there's always someone who doesn't get back to the coach on time. But you're on your way to Wembley, so you laugh it off through gritted teeth.

A better option would be drugs, at least heavy-duty sleeping pills to make the four hours on the road fly by. But through drooping eyelids, waving to other Alex fans on coaches, in cars, vans and even on the back of motorbikes was irresistible. I took photos of fancy-dress fans, of the flags being waved at Watford Gap services, and even made a mental note of the numbers milling around the concourse (for the record, it was about 500 when we stopped off). I felt like a trainspotter wearing football colours. In the background I was still dad. The lads are no longer little kids, but any journey is arduous. And they nagged!

HOW FAR TO GO?

The most common travel question was asked as each junction or landmark was passed. I reeled off countless useless, boring "dad" facts, observations from so many treks along those motorways, usually when heading to see a game. Floodlights and tops of stands were highlighted, although the blurred specs in the distance impressed none of my lot. They even scoffed at my favourite hitching points, places where I'd grabbed lifts home to make sure I could see games at Gresty Road in my youth. When we swept around the north edge of London I was tempted to tell the little horrors that it was Birmingham, as they would have been none the wiser. But I didn't. I was too excited myself as those famous skyscrapers started to appear in the distance.

The coach dropped us outside Wembley, which was fair enough I suppose. But that meant a lengthy walk, as the independent "Fordy" travellers had made a beeline for one particular watering hole. That was our rendezvous point. It was already hot, less than T-shirt weather. The kids wanted food, the wife fancied some sight-seeing, but I was ready for a pint. So off we went, up the hill away from the stadium, asking random strangers the best route to take. Then other Alex fans decked out in red and white made it obvious that we were on the right track; it just took forever. The sweat was pouring when we eventually arrived at our pre-match destination.

The Green Man Hotel was the nominated Alex boozer, a massive old building that looked like a house with multiple extensions and conservatories. It was slap bang in the middle of a residential area, but somehow felt secluded. Mature planting and towering old trees kept it screened, and with thousands of Alex supporters expected, it was a good job, as the neighbours would be shielded from the commotion.

The police like to keep things tidy, and being able to segregate supporters in advance keeps the chance of trouble down to a minimum; although this wasn't a day for falling out. Everyone was in celebratory mood and up for a laugh. Enjoying the day through to 5pm was all-important. Beyond that, well, one set of fans would be crying in their beer deep into the evening. There was no chance it was going to be us.

At the pub a fast-food vendor was already doing a brisk trade; dodgy matchday merchandise was on offer from another van, and a couple of shady looking fellas were furtively asking if anyone needed tickets. We didn't, but it was tempting to ask how much the black market was booming and whether the Alex stock had gone up.

It was still early, at least in terms of a "normal" matchday. We made our way to the back entrance of the pub at about 12.30pm. The noise that hit us was deafening. Plumes of BBQ smoke curled invitingly all around us, and the first football chants were being orchestrated. It was a sprawling mish-mash of gardens, some decking and paving stones, a huge expanse that should have been green, brown and grey. Instead it was red and white. Replica shirts, flags, scarves and already cherry-red sunburnt bodies - everywhere! It was jaw-dropping, the most Crewe supporters I'd ever seen congregated in and around one pub. Almost festival-like, people were dancing with drinks, raising them high into the air as each chorus of song reached a crescendo. Some were barefoot; T-shirts were wrapped around waists, and other items of unnecessary clothing were already discarded. I could have watched this wonderful mayhem all day.

Getting a pint was another matter. Inside the dark, cool interior of the pub the queues for beers were three and four deep. Behind us more fans were still pouring through the doors. In they came, every face lit up, excited and delighted to be part of the experience. It was £4 per pint, cooking lager and wishy-washy bitter, but nobody seemed to care. Fives, tens and twenties were handed over, exchanged for more and more flimsy pots sloshing with alcohol. And still they came, peeling off coats and sweaters as the temperature soared inside and out. Before we left with our drinks it was like an oven.

Outside we battled through the crowds, saying hello to friendly faces and some people we had not seen since the last play-off final against Brentford. We had all aged, and yet eyes were alive with youthful hope. Once again I had that feeling of invincibility. The Alex would win; no doubt about it.

THREE-NIL!

A blast from the past called out to me, thumbs up as he turned to offer his prediction to others. Most were the same, on edge but quietly confident. The unbeaten run was going to continue, it had to.

Then the sunshine, the glorious shafts of golden light that hit us when we made it out of the bar. The double-doors led to a wooden canopy, a trellis of sorts that connected different sections of the pub exterior. Rambling ivy draped over the frame, offering some welcome shade. In and out people flooded. Some looked out for friends; others were desperately searching for youngsters that had wandered off. They were all okay, playing in one of several groups already kicking a beach ball, disrupting adults trying to drink and chat. But nobody cared; it was Wembley. The kids could do what they liked. It was their day too.

Then I saw Ray, Marie, Katie and Dean. It was coming together. They'd arrived earlier, on the more direct "drinkers" bus, straight to London and parked up at the pub itself. Ray looked glazed already, massive smile, lager going down like pop. Then Darren, Amanda, Andy, Shaun and Alan, other mates I'd not seen for a while, Jonesy, Tim, kids I didn't recognise, older faces from my London days, Wilko, big Simes, Graham and many more. Everyone was smiling.

WE ARE THE, WE'RE THE RAILWAYMEN...

More chanting started up and an inflatable flew inches over our heads. It was like the best days on the Popside, a noise that only hundreds of supporters can make when they come together. There were people squeezed into every conceivable space. There was too much to take in.

City office blocks filled the backdrop, two large marquees doubled-up as shelter and temporary beer points, and another jumbled line of thirsty drinkers formed as the patio bar opened its doors for business. It felt like the whole of Crewe was on holiday, basking in the sun, happy chatter everywhere, so much anticipation of the game that was a couple of hours away.

That get-together, the reunion of footy mates on such a massive scale, is like the annual family meal at Christmas. There's so much to say, too many people to greet, almost impossible to grab more than a passing word with some. And yet you have a million lines of thought, minute details that you'd only share with those allowed into that inner circle. You've bottled it up for a season, longer in some cases. And it's not the same at work, or with "real" family who don't share the Alex passion. You can't tell them how you feel, what the day means to you. But here, amidst like-minded fools that have lived the same terrace life, you want to pour out your every thought. It's a comfort blanket, a desire to gain reassurance from those who genuinely understand you. And they do. Sometimes it just takes a nod. That's enough. There is a common bond, a connection, a secret code that does not need to be solved. We were one that afternoon.

Then "the Conga" started. A staggering line of ten set out, a minibus full that looked as though they'd bypassed the drinking laws of matchday travel. Then fifteen, twenty and soon thirty nipped in and out, around tables, grabbing new members as they danced through the crowds that cheered their every step. Beer sloshed, people fell but everyone loved it. Drums controlled the beat but the rambling chain had a mind of its own. They stopped by a group of traditional pub tables and the singing proper began. I leapt onto a seat to take a picture; there was no need to co-ordinate the group shot, as the rabble waved automatically and raised their glasses in unison. Smiles widened to greet every camera and mobile phone that flashed to capture those heady moments. It was magic.

So many photos were taken that day. It would be wonderful to stitch them together, a million viewpoints from so many different angles; friends, colours, faces, poses, moments, kisses, banners, beers and beaming smiles. That mosaic would be spectacular, but technology ensured that so many of those snaps reached the masses in seconds. People passed by with phones bolted to ears, forwarding those images, relaying the scenes to friends en route, to family back home and to mates still trying to hook up. Finding anyone was increasingly hard. The numbers rose steadily and you wondered if the flow would ever ease. Every blade of grass was covered, no room to sit, just body-to-body as far as the eye could see.

The second round of beers was a real challenge. I chose the outdoor bar that had an impressive conveyor belt in operation. The staff didn't stop. Kegs delivered golden liquid without pausing, extra foamy because it was rushed. The barrels hadn't settled and the heat didn't help. Nobody minded the spillages. Each pint was flung on the bar as notes and coins swelled the till. And then again, another fistful of beers headed out, more thirsty punters replacing those who moved on. Cheeky mates called out to lads already in the queue, turning orders of four into fourteen in the blink of an eye. All around [plastic] glass collectors hurried, desperately trying to keep pace with the turnover. Rough estimates suggest that at its peak around three thousand Alex fans were milling around that watering hole. It was organised chaos, but still it flowed, yet more bodies squeezing through the doors, hunting out toilets and immediately regretting it; they were a mess!

As I peeled away with lagers in hand Steve Jones appeared. Everyone wanted a piece of the former Alex striker. There were handshakes, slaps on the back and appeals for him to once again return to the Crewe side. He laughed along, swept away with a tide of compliments and stories that supporters thrust upon him. He was a fan that day, one of us, another voice to roar the side on to glory. And there it was again. "Jonesy" was also confident, in no doubt that we would lift the play-off trophy later that afternoon. It was now only an hour away.

We needed to get moving, and yet that all-dayer lure is irresistible on occasions bathed in sunshine. There were too many stories to swap, conversations to finish and laughs to be had. The good times were relived over and over, not a single mention of York '93 when "old" Wembley proved to be such a downer.

WE ARE GOING UP, WE ARE GOING UP...

The Alex choir continued to warm up ahead of kick-off. The words bounced off the pub and the trees swayed. Everyone felt it, a surge in belief as the action ticked another minute closer. The more sensible fans started to move on, a twenty-minute walk to the stadium ahead of them. We grabbed another beer and lapped up more banter. My youngest headed off with his mate, helping to sell some one-off T-shirts printed for the final. He disappeared into a sea of colour, tops from every season, ducking under the banners and flags that were now flapping all around. On the far side, the tail-end of the Conga culminated in a last dance, bodies grappling to stay atop one of the wooden tables. They fell into a delighted heap, still singing, some managing to save dregs of beer as they landed.

Then, almost as one, the majority finished drinks, grabbed bags, kids and wives, checked tickets yet again and thanked the pub staff for their hospitality. The army began to march. It was less than twenty five minutes to kick-off, we were cutting it fine, but the searing heat didn't hamper the quick pace down the hill towards the stadium. It was time.

AND POWELL SCORED!

Putting the play-off final words together I wondered how I should tackle the overall package. There was the journey, the pre-match stuff and of course the action itself. Nick Powell convinced me to split it up. Not the man himself, of course, but the contribution he made. It had to enjoy space on its own, away from the other distractions that made up the incredible day out to Wembley. We've covered the restless "are we there yet" queries from the kids, and the beery preparations before kick-off; so now the main course.

First, I will make the assumption that 99% of readers sampled the delights of Wembley 2012. This is a recap, a refresher, something to rekindle fond memories. There would have to be some fantastical excuses to have missed our first jolly to the national stadium in fifteen years. A family wedding in the Caribbean would be good enough; or maybe rowing across the Atlantic on a solo charity expedition, that would have sufficed. But nothing else; you had to be there. For my lads and many others it was the first time in their young lifetimes that the opportunity had arisen. And based on the previous few years of turmoil, nobody would dare guess when the next glitzy occasion would be.

So I don't really need to describe the walk up Wembley Way, past the posters, statues, scarf sellers and fast-food vans. Unlike the '97 experience, we didn't walk down the stadium approach. We caught the view about ten minutes before kick-off, but looking the other way as thousands were still meandering towards the venue from the tube station. We'd come from the pub, from the other direction.

The hike from *The Green Man* takes you to the far side of the concourse, and I had another pre-match complication. There was a late hook-up with a Scandinavian Alex fan, Helge Gjerstad. We'd swapped messages on Twitter; it was a rare chance for him to see the Alex in the flesh. But he'd struggled to get a ticket, and when details were finally sorted it was too late to post it out from the club. So I bought an extra one and arranged a handover at the pub, so Helge could also meet a few of the lads.

But best laid plans and all that… you guessed it: his flight, train and other transport options were delayed. It was 50:50 if he'd make it on time. Then a late text arrived. He was en route, but unlikely to get there to have a pint. So outside the Alex section at Wembley was the best bet to complete the transaction. It worked out perfectly. The profile picture was enough to track him down, and with a few handshakes the deal was done. The global Alex gathering was ready for some match action.

WOW!

Inside the new-build is breath-taking. We're not used to fancy hi-tech gadgets at Gresty Road, so the scan and swipe at the electronic gates was befuddling for some. Security guards frisked, cameras followed our every move and barcodes recorded our arrival. What struck me was the scale of everything. There was no ceiling; at least that's how it seemed. It went on forever. And it wasn't all concrete. Fabric banners advertised the finalists, others promoted forthcoming events. The bars and drinking areas were sleek, beautifully finished, still gleaming as though the fitters had just completed the job. It was impressive. And so were the prices! Burger and chips didn't leave much change from ten quid. Pints, for those wanting additional liquid fuel, were an eye-watering £4.50 each. Oh, but there was free water from the fountain if you didn't mind joining a two-hundred yard queue!

But all of that commercial stuff is quickly forgotten when you walk out to the main arena just a few metres from the bars and other facilities. It's a slick approach, no steps, just a steady incline. But it was slow progress, as the trickle of fans making their way to the seating area kept stopping. They were gawping, just as we did when the vast expanse of turf appeared. The Wembley playing surface is like a bowling green. Like a perfectly still lake as far as the eye can see; it grabs you. "Keep moving," a nearby steward encouraged. We did, but there are a million details to absorb as you take the steps to your seat, ticket clutched in hand, watching the smiling faces, the flags waving, the dancing inflatables out on the pitch, and of course the players going through final warm-ups.

We'd left it all quite late. The Alex squad was huddled about fifty metres away, the last instructions from Captain Dave Artell being dished out to players keen to get started. A quick team roar and then they broke free, darting across the pitch to take up their positions. I waved to Alex snapper Pete Warburton who was making his way around the pitch. He'd been taking photos of the fans; capturing those special moments, pre-match expressions telling a thousand stories, so much hope and expectation etched on faces ahead of the game.

It was sweltering. My daft floppy hat wasn't looking so silly by now, as others grabbed programmes to shield their eyes. Ray wrapped a scarf around his head to stop sunburn, and Ritchie decided to shift his family to the shaded side of the ground. Andy, Paul and Alan were too busy singing to worry. The stewards, though, were tremendous. They handed out water to youngsters and offered to relocate anyone struggling with the temperature. All around us tops came off, beer bellies on show like a day trip to the seaside.

The heat helped to focus minds. It left little time to worry about the match. But in those final seconds, the tense moments before the kick-off, you cannot help but panic a little. What if our unbridled confidence was unfounded? What if Cheltenham sussed us out and had a master plan to outwit our players? Those fabulous eighteen unbeaten games would count for nothing. But losing was never an option. I looked out to men in the centre-circle and hoped that they shared my confidence.

GAME ON!

Over fifteen thousand chattering Crewe voices hushed and watched as the first passes were completed. The game of chess was under way. It was down to the players now to execute carefully prepared passages of play. Steve Davis and his opposite number, Mark Yates, took up positions in the technical area. The pleasantries were over. The winner would take all. And then we sang...

Those opening minutes are always the worst. You wonder whether the Alex will start brightly, if they will grab an early goal. Will the defenders panic and is the referee going to be tough on niggling fouls? Questions, questions, questions! Of course we had momentum on our side. We had long forgotten what defeat tasted like. Few dared to say it, but we were invincible that day. I'd replayed countless scenarios in my mind leading up to the match. Each time it was the same. We were too strong for Cheltenham, our passing too slick, our forwards too mobile, midfielders far too intelligent and the defence was fifteen feet tall. Steve Phillips had gloves the size of dustbin lids. This was our day.

The first doubts fill your head when the opposition attacks. That Wembley pitch looks massive, far too much ground to cover. The players look like toy figures. I scanned left, right and then back to Phillips in goal. Everything was set up perfectly. Harry Davis was back in position, Artell alongside Adam Dugdale in the middle, with Matt Tootle on the right. We looked solid, up for it, ready for anything they could throw at us.

I had assessed the line-up several times ahead of kick-off, but in those early minutes I had to look again. Apart from Phillips and Artell at the back, the rest were lads brought through the Alex academy. Moving forward through the team, in addition to Davis and Tootle, Kelvin Mellor, Ashley Westwood, Luke Murphy, Nick Powell, AJ Leitch-Smith and Byron

Moore were all home-grown kids, many of them from the town of Crewe itself. Somehow we knew it meant more to them; and as a collective there was no way they would let the opportunity slip through their fingers. This was the biggest day of their young lives.

The Alex didn't dominate the opening quarter of an hour but there was a great vibe throughout our section. Nobody looked concerned, even when Cheltenham stole possession. Looking up to the right, along from the Royal Box to our "end" it was a blaze of red and white, although the Alex were forced to wear the black "away" kit. In terms of tickets sold, Cheltenham were in the minority and the volume from the Crewe end soon confirmed our numerical dominance. There was a steady rumble of noise around us, some songs gaining momentum as the lyrics spread to the more vocal fans.

Then a quick throw-in deep inside the Cheltenham half found Tootle. Under pressure he worked a clever one-two with Mellor. He controlled, turned towards goal and released the ball to Powell on the edge of the "D". The Alex magician had a bag of his tricks at his disposal, all perfectly executed across the season. Everyone had seen them and knew exactly what he was capable of. But not what followed seconds later. Hundreds of Alex fans will have missed the moment. A glance over the shoulder, a single word with friends, or a bite on a burger - anything more than the blink of an eye will have deprived them of the most sublime moment in real time. Powell took Mellor's firm pass in his stride. As usual his first touch was faultless. What we saw from the far end was a clever turn and looping shot that was just too accurate, too fast and too hot for the Cheltenham 'keeper to handle. The lad flapped, dived for the cameras but never got close to the wonder strike...

AND POWELL SCORED!

Closer analysis shows a subtle dummy draw two defenders; his first touch then took the ball in the opposite direction. Another defender spotted the danger and moved in, but the ball had already left Powell's boot. Even the Alex players dotted around the box were under his spell. Leitch-Smith made a darting run, hopeful that his strike partner might release the ball into his path. But the decision had been made. The trigger was pulled by a crack marksman. It was a millisecond of genius.

The goal took everyone by surprise. The immediate reaction was to look to the referee and his assistant. It was too good to be true. There would be an offside, a foul or some kind of encroachment to spoil our moment of bliss. All of this happened in that single blink of an eye. Some were punching the air and waving tops and scarves, while others prayed that the goal would stand. Had the Alex really had taken the lead? But there was no dramatic objection. Even the Cheltenham players looked on in awe. Their heads dropped. Powell was better than all of them. They knew it. That moment of brilliance killed them off.

ONE-NIL!

On the touchline Davis was alone. He was already dancing towards the Crewe end, fist in the air, trying hard to look professional but desperate to let his emotions explode in unison with the fans. I'm sure he wanted to do a dramatic José Mourinho impression, to race the length of the touchline and slide towards the corner flag. But the game was still young. He kept his cool while we cavorted like deranged idiots. Five years of frustration went pop. We all let rip, bouncing up and down in the seats, some racing down the gangways and others jumping on mates' shoulders. The stewards stood to attention, keen to monitor the situation. At Wembley there is a wide expanse of netting that keeps supporters away from the pitch. That's probably a good thing, as a visit to the national stadium is a very special one-off, and people do strange things when under the influence of a few pints. It was tempting, very tempting, and I never criticise those who choose to race onto the playing surface to join their heroes in celebration. It's breaking the law, for sure, but those moments of euphoria, that head-rush that comes hand-in-hand with a goal is enough to send even the most dour supporter down the path of criminality. Okay, so it is wrong to condone pitch invading, but who wouldn't want to spend even a few seconds with Powell after he had just converted perhaps the best goal in the new stadium's history?

The goal was amazing, but it was just the first of many incidents and talking points. The next came two minutes after the restart. The Alex defence wasn't napping, but an incisive pass straight through the middle found Cheltenham striker Jeff Goulding unmarked. He was desperate to catch us unaware and banged a sweet right-footed shot over Phillips and onto the bar. The Alex chanting stopped dead in its tracks; the ball looped up and bounced dangerously around the six-yard area. Defenders scrambled into position - blocking, holding and shirt-tugging anyone in red. They did enough. The moment passed and we all started to sing again.

That pre-match confidence started to return. You could see it etched on the faces of every Alex player, especially close-up when we defended corners in that first half. They knew what they were doing. They were in charge. There was no hoof-ball, no arguing with the referee. They just got on with things. Even when Phillips picked the ball out of his net a little later, there was barely a flutter. The assistant stood motionless, flag raised in the air until he was noticed. We'd seen him instantly. Even the officials were on our side!

But Cheltenham came on strong. They forced a cracking save from the Alex stopper, and we all winced as the ball twice flew past the goal and into the crowd. They meant business, but the Crewe rearguard performed heroics. Again and again we watched perfectly-timed tackles and blocks - heads, knees and feet thrown in where it hurts. We even cleared twice off the goal line! Phillips showed his experience, holding the ball a few precious seconds longer than required each time he caught a cross or smothered a shot. Cheltenham protested; the referee waved them away and nodded to the Alex goalkeeper. It was gamesmanship.

The Alex never sat back though. The young lads didn't know how. They passed and probed, tried short one-twos and looked long down the wings when Moore or Powell sped off into space. What I remember most was the composure. Westwood and Murphy in particular ran the game. They didn't flap or panic once. If they lost the ball they scuttled into position and won it back. Then they'd start again, perfecting the pass that didn't quite reach its intended target moments earlier. There was no fear.

Without running away with it, we looked comfortable against Cheltenham. But this was not like the annihilation of Brentford back in '97. That day, that fabulous sunny day at "old" Wembley was non-stop Crewe. Many described it as the most one-sided 1-0 win they had ever seen. And yet it was tense; we remained fearful of a Brentford surge until the final whistle.

It was the same against Cheltenham. Only a second goal could now settle the nerves and confirm our superiority. As the first forty five minutes came to a close, it was still anyone's game.

***

The clock struck 4pm and the sun finally started to relent a little. The Alex players came out refreshed, and kicked towards the rosy-cheeked Crewe fans. It was about to become a thrilling second half. Cheltenham had to throw everything at us, and they did. There was more hectic defending, but the bond that had developed between those Alex players was evident for all to see. The spirit was magnificent. If one lost the ball, two others harried and chased until it was safe. When a player was under pressure, one, two and three stepped up to give him options. The manager, coaches and fans could not have asked for more.

Dugdale in particular led by example. He stuck his head in to protect the Alex goal numerous times, and midway through the second half he almost grabbed himself a goal. A tantalising Westwood free-kick curled over and beyond the Cheltenham defence. Duggy tried to steer the ball past the goalkeeper when a good, old-fashioned thump would have probably done the trick. The Robins stopper, Scott Brown, threw himself at man and ball; Dugdale was denied by the finest margin.

Had another Alex strike gone in then Cheltenham would have surrendered. The blistering heat was taking its toll, and for some the dreaded cramp set in. The players took on water when they could, and the referee was sensible in letting them dash to the touchline during breaks in play. All games should be like that. It can only help the overall experience, and certainly the health of those out in the sun.

The game continued to flow, end-to-end, but it was Crewe that dominated play and possession - at least in my head! I was too wrapped up in the wonderful atmosphere to appreciate how often we had to soak up pressure. I looked away when Cheltenham came close and dismissed how many corners they won. In fact, it was only when I got back home later that evening and watched the highlights that I realised how tight the game had been. Cheltenham created plenty of superb chances. They had eight corners to our six, and unleashed more shots at goal than Crewe - although many of their efforts were off-target. And perhaps that was the key: the Alex had the quality when it mattered.

On eighty minutes Davis made a bold substitution. He took off Powell, the goal scorer, a fans' favourite who could change a game in a second. You could hear the concern amongst the Crewe supporters, all wondering if the rookie manager was making a huge mistake. The job wasn't done. We needed the second goal. The problem was that the youngster was tiring. He'd given 100% and was making a few mistakes. Several passes were wayward. He was dead on his feet, the intense heat claiming another victim. On came another kid, 18-year-old Max Clayton, yet another off the Alex production line and an England U19 partner of Powell's. As the swap was completed every Crewe fan applauded, Davis slapped his player on the back and Powell sat down with his squad mates. He'd made a significant mark on Wembley history.

What happened a few minutes after the switch was perfect. Clayton played his part, peeling off and dragging a defender with him as the Alex attacked. Moore received a pass out wide, took his time assessing the options, then darted inside and threatened a run on goal. He didn't; instead he stalled, pushed the ball wide before spraying an unexpected pass to Leitch-Smith. I half expected a quick shot, but as Moore created space on the right-hand side of the penalty area he received the ball back at his feet completely unmarked. He took just two paces to adjust, and then fired a low shot across the face of goal.

YESSSSS!

The noise was deafening, but like a clap of thunder there was a momentary lull as we all watched Moore slip as he connected with the ball. It was going wide, at least from our angle. But the 'keeper once again flapped, stretched as though his life depended on it, and rolled into a crumpled heap by his right-hand post. The ball was still settling into the netting.

That's when the party started, at least amongst the Alex fans. There was still ten minutes to play after the referee's inevitable additional minutes were added, but the Cheltenham players were spent. The body language and look on their faces said beaten men. And yet they had supporters at the other end of the stadium that had paid good money and arrived with hope in their hearts. So they had to play on; even though all but the most optimistic Robins fans knew that their promotion dream was over. The fallen players were scattered around the penalty area following Moore's foray deep into their territory. They hauled themselves up, weary, shattered and heartbroken. It only takes a second to score a goal, but they knew it wasn't happening for them that afternoon. They would not have scored if they had played on until midnight.

One substitution that must get a mention is the introduction of Lee Bell in stoppage time. There was no risk, the official was already checking his watch, and by now Cheltenham had all but given up. But Belly deserved his moment in the Wembley sun. Perhaps Davis knew that he would be one of the players released that summer, and getting the tough-tackling midfielder a little game time was a thank you for services rendered. Maybe I'm reading too much into the gesture; the gaffer was probably trying to use up a few extra seconds and frustrate the opponents further. Whatever... Bell played at Wembley for Crewe Alexandra.

The referee, Craig Pawson, was our best friend that day. He'd kept tabs on the cynical fouls, awarded free-kicks fairly and kept his notebook stowed away in his top pocket. There were no bookings. Two honest teams played out a blinder, but there could be only one winner. Right on queue he pursed his lips and blew three short blasts to end the match. Cheltenham players fell to the floor while the Alex lads jumped into each other's arms. Men who had been fit to collapse moments earlier found fresh legs as they raced to the crowd, scanning the many faces for friends and family. They stood before us, waving to the supporters who had adopted them as their own. Then they wrestled with Davis and Bakes, fabulous horseplay, spraying the duo with water bottles. By now, they had long since dropped their stern managerial veneers. They all wanted to skip around the pitch, shout and yell alongside thousands of Crewe relations they did not know but wanted to treat like family.

And then the spoils, the presentation of the trophy. The players climbed steps that seemed to wind on and up forever. It was easier watching their progress on the big screen above our heads. Intimate close-ups captured their emotions, and we were part of the moment. Each player was cheered, and when that play-off cup was hoisted high above Artell's head we all danced and hugged like lunatics, drunk on success.

Down below the fans watched wide-eyed, some with tears streaming down their face. For all its hype, Wembley really is a wondrous place when you win. In those moments after the players received medals the pitch was transformed into a Disney fairytale set. A platform was whisked onto the grass. Gigantic flags were dragged into position. Streamers and confetti filled the sky and music shook the stadium foundations. Hundreds of security stewards in sunglasses guarded the touchline; the players taking the place of movie stars. We sang each and every name as they passed the trophy around.

The Wembley facilities had been upgraded, but there was a definite feeling of déjà vu. In fact, I remember the May '97 celebrations as though it was yesterday. The blaring music (M People), dry ice, baking sunshine and delirious players are still fresh in my mind. This time it was "Paradise" by Coldplay, a tune that can't fail to bring back more wonderful memories when we look back on this day in years to come. It was another sweltering afternoon and the celebrations were equally lavish. But there were two differences: this time we knew what to expect. We'd "done" a Wembley win before. We had lived life in the higher divisions. Another noticeable change was the hardware on show. Almost every supporter clutched a mobile phone, catching personal memories, calling friends who might have mocked over the years, and posting details to social media so every man and his dog could share our joy.

Despite all this it was still hard to comprehend. In six months Davis had unlocked something, sparked desire that had been missing and got levels of performance from players who had been idling under previous managers. We will never know why, or how, but after three miserable seasons in the basement the Alex were back in the division that I, and others, believe to be "our" level.

Dario Gradi, the master of previous successes, was there, away from the management team but watching on from the seats high up above. I wonder what he made of the turnaround. I'd like to think that he was consumed with pride, not jealousy or regrets. That's not his style being bitter. He was probably looking forward to Monday morning, getting back to work with one age group or another. His driving force was always football. Whatever fans thought of the man, he had been responsible for ten of the players who had just triumphed on the pitch that day. It was his work, his long-term vision, his patience with lads that needed his vast experience. He just did not have his hands on the trophy this time.

One final mention must go to Steve Holland. His demise at Crewe was well documented earlier in this book, but against Cheltenham he was one of Crewe Alexandra's guests of honour in the main entertainment lounge. That was a nice touch by the club. He did a lot for the Alex. Whatever happened in his final spell as manager, we should never forget that he played a huge part at the academy alongside Gradi.

On the coach home, the effort put in by supporters young and old was evident. We had all played our part and were drained - just like the players, but for different reasons. Sunstroke, beers and shouting is never a good combination! Some slept, others flicked through pictures taken on phones and cameras, and a few relived the day with softly-spoken chat. I had a *Sentinel* newspaper piece to file, awkwardly typed on the tiny keypad of my mobile phone. With the last dregs of battery life I clicked send. And then I dozed, catching up on the sleep I'd missed the previous night. I pretended not to hear my youngest ask "are we home yet" as the coach slipped onto the M1...

PAINT POT

The planning for League One started as the bottles and party poppers were swept away after a crazy night of celebrations in the main lounge back at Gresty Road. Hundreds of fans had waited patiently for the official coach, and then swarmed the players who had done the business at Wembley. Then valves popped, shackles were removed and disciplined athletes abused their bodies with drink and cake until they could take no more. It was a one-off, the culmination of six intense months. They had achieved the seemingly impossible.

Steve Davis joined Neil Baker for speeches, beers and the customary karaoke, but the pre-season was already on the manager's mind. Within days he had to deliver the grim news to those who would be released. The annual "cull" was something everyone at the club dreaded. Men who had been familiar faces for two, three and more seasons would no longer turn up at training, or say hello to staff at the club's offices. But football is a tough business; the need to recruit fresh blood was pressing. Davis could not put additional strain on the limited wage budget. He had to make space to give himself room to manoeuvre in the transfer market. Some of the players earmarked for the chop, if we are blunt and honest about it, were probably not good enough for the higher division. The Alex could not afford to carry surplus passengers.

At the other end of the scale, there was always the spectre of player sales. The Alex never block a transfer, especially if it is in the best interests of one of its graduates. But that doesn't help the manager as he prepares for the new season. After promotion had sunk in, one concern was the imminent departure of Nick Powell. The rumours of a move to any one of ten Premier League clubs had been circulating since before Christmas. His exit was a formality, but we still didn't know where he'd hang his boots. The second the ball left his foot at Wembley every Alex supporter knew that his fate was sealed, if it wasn't already. We just hoped that the goal added another million to his price tag. That wouldn't replace the player, but it would soften the blow and allow Davis to plan around the rest of his squad. It finally happened in July when the Crewe wonder kid signed for Manchester United.

Everything was set for Ashley Westwood to become the team's shining light, but a late move to Aston Villa made things additionally complex. Someone else could now emerge as the team's dominant force. That man would be Luke Murphy. But what two high-profile sales meant was that

Davis and Baker had to rethink the priorities. The bread-and-butter season would be about consolidation, no more. That's what they planned for, and sensibly too.

So another distraction was required. Now football fans have Christmas, Easter and birthdays like other "normal" people, but we also have our own code and staggered highlights that keep us interested from one season to the next (unless there's Euro or World Cup action to stop us snoozing the summer away). I'd have to say that the release of the fixture list tops mine, closely followed by transfer deadline day. But this season would be about knock-out action. The draw for the FA Cup is always enthralling, with most of us wanting an unusual away day at some far-flung non-league outfit. But the most famous club competition in the world was beyond us. We had to drop our expectations somewhat.

No disrespect, but some ten paces behind the League Cup is the Football League Trophy. In the mid-1980s it was the Associate Members' Cup, and then from 1992 they jumped on the branding bandwagon and gave it real "league" credibility. Of course with that came varied sponsorship deals, and the early ones (like Freight Rover, Sherpa Vans, Leyland DAF, Autoglass, Auto Windscreens and LDV Vans) revolved around the automotive industry.

I'm being somewhat disingenuous, as for many years I have thought that this tournament was a realistic option if Crewe Alexandra wanted to win a cup. But even teams from our level dismissed it. Look at the crowds and it's apparent that most supporters also considered it unworthy. Some of the smaller clubs have used it to blood their younger players, fans have continued to attend in hundreds rather than thousands, and the finals have been played out to smaller gatherings than would attend the entire weekend of the Nantwich Jazz Festival. It has been a competition that most scoff at, and the winning teams over the years have gained little credibility.

***

Looking back, I still think that we should have won the competition in 2003 (sponsored by LDV Vans that year). As a Championship side for several seasons we didn't take part in the Football League Trophy between 1997 and 2002. But in the season spent back in the third tier we suddenly found another date in the diary. Crewe thumped Mansfield 4-0 at Field Mill in the opening round, then comfortably despatched Blackpool 2-0 at Gresty Road at the second stage. So far, so good!

In early December, Alex fans received an early Christmas present. We went goal-crazy at home to lowly Doncaster in the northern quarter-final. There were five goal scorers in the 8-0 win, and what an illustrious list it was! Dean Ashton claimed the matchball with three; Rodney Jack grabbed two; and David Vaughan, Kenny Lunt and Steve Jones scored one apiece. This was a team with bags of experience and phenomenal fire power. If Rob Hulse had been fit the referee might have been forced to stop the contest. It was an awesome display. The team oozed confidence; the Alex were also en route to promotion.

So the northern semi-final against Shrewsbury in January 2003 was a cute distraction, a chance to give fringe lads a run-out and ensure that players like Hulse returned to full-fitness ready for the final third of an important season. Before kick-off, Crewe had lost only one of the previous seventeen matches. Our opponents, by comparison, had lost five of their last seventeen games; the most recent a 4-0 reverse at home to Chelsea in the FA Cup. As a club from the fourth tier, they were second favourites going into the game against Crewe.

At Gay Meadow (Shrewsbury's former ground prior to 2007) the away end was packed. There was huge expectation ahead of the Shropshire-Cheshire derby. It was an opportunity to run up another cricket score for us. But Shrewsbury hit first; and they doubled the lead two minutes into the second half. We were gobsmacked. So at 2-0 down there were rumblings of discontent. Did we really want to win the cup? Ashton was off the pace, and the determined Shrews kept the Alex clear of their box. They dug in and parked the bus. I remember standing there in a trance. It was a bizarre sensation. The Alex played at half speed, seemingly disinterested. As the game wore on, I wondered if the team would ever burst into life.

They did, and it was Hulse back in the side who gave the Alex a lifeline. The tempo increased. We camped on the edge of the Shrewsbury area. Shots, crosses and trademark one-twos suggested we'd draw level... but there was no way through. The home side wanted it more. Perhaps manager Dario Gradi should have made changes sooner, freshened the midfield and attack as we moved into the final phase of the match. But he didn't, not until the 76th minute. That was after Shrewsbury had pillaged two more goals in a five-minute burst. We were dead and buried. Ashton's late strike was mere consolation as we lost 4-2. We were gutted. Another opportunity to win a cup was thrown away.

There was another season that generated hope. In February 2007 the Alex made it to the northern final against Doncaster. A thrilling 3-3 draw at home was matched for entertainment by a controversial 2-3 defeat away at the fabulous Keepmoat Stadium. In the second leg, the Alex threw away a two-goal lead and then had to do battle with the referee. He awarded a contentious spot kick that was taken twice. That levelled the scores before Doncaster grabbed a very late winner. Alex substitute Michael Higdon still had chance to equalise, but his effort was harshly ruled offside. The match official won no friends from Cheshire that night!

For me, although we progressed further, that 2007/08 season was not quite the same. The cavalier forwards of 2003 did not make it as far in the tournament, but they had promised so much. At their best they were thrilling. They should have gone on to win it - and in style. But the wait continued.

***

Fast-forward to the 2012/13 season, and I believe that Steve Davis saw the competition as a way to endear himself to Crewe fans forever. Matching Gradi's considerable achievements was the most daunting of tasks, but the Football League Trophy was something missing from the Gresty Road trophy cabinet. From 2006 the competition got a makeover and emerged with a lick of gloss courtesy of Johnstone's Paint (the JPT). With it, fans' perception of the tournament started to change. As the gulf between elite and bottom feeders - rich and poor - has widened and the top-flight has all but pulled up the ladders, the rest have realised that any trophy is worth winning. It can generate extra revenue, and it helps to keep the squad players fit. A winning run can also inspire the team to further success in the all-important league action; and who does not enjoy a day out at Wembley?

Also of interest is the route to the final. At most, it takes seven games to lift the Johnstone's Paint trophy; two regionalised early rounds, then quarter, semi and area finals (the latter over two legs); and then Wembley, where north take on south to determine the overall winner. It can be that simple.

So in October 2012, with the League One campaign so-so, I started to take notice of the competition. For starters, the Alex enjoyed a bye in the first round. The action proper began (coincidently) away at Shrewsbury in front of half-decent crowd of 2,063. On the afternoon of the match I toyed with the idea of travelling over, but a late finish at work and the fact that I was starving convinced me to make it a date with the trusty DAB radio. So I settled down with Graham McGarry and Radio Stoke. There is little point reliving action from the airwaves, although with our roving Crewe reporter things can get pretty lively. It's dramatic enough when we concede a goal, gift a penalty to the opposition or have a player sent off; but when we score - WOW! Our Graham gets very excited, sometimes rivalling the most OTT South American commentator. It's a great experience. You live every kick, get the statistics you miss sat up in the stands, and of course you can sup a glass of wine as you soak in the bath; decadence!

What impressed me as I enjoyed the early exchanges of the Shrewsbury match was that Davis played a strong side. He took the competition seriously from that first game. In fact, it was the same starting line-up that had beaten Hartlepool 2-1 in the league a few days earlier. I suspect he wanted to get some momentum going, as the season had so far been patchy. But I also think he fancied having a real run at the JPT as it was one competition that had out-foxed his predecessor, Dario Gradi.

That night didn't kick-start an unbeaten run comparable with his first season, but Davis and his players shrugged off the early-season blues and finally adapted to life after Powell and Westwood. They beat Shrewsbury 2-1 and looked forward instead of back. There were nine league games before the next round and they lost just three. Solid wins over Swindon, Doncaster and Crawley were highlights, plus a scintillating 3-3 draw away at Sheffield United. There was even a comfortable 4-1 win in round one of the FA Cup at home to Wycombe Wanderers. It was more than satisfactory progress for supporters who had feared the worst with the team's playmakers gone. There was no complacency, however, as injuries and suspensions were always likely to have a bearing on the second half of the season.

At the heart of most plays was Luke Murphy. He blossomed and seemed to grow a foot in height with the additional responsibility of the captain's armband. He also scored goals. By December he had five to his name, netting in both the JPT win at Shrewsbury and the Wycombe romp. The manager also played a joker: the loan system. He brought Lauri Dalla Valle in from Premier League Fulham, a three-month deal that paid off from day one. He shot four in his first five games to keep the Alex goal count rising.

The steady revival continued at home to Doncaster, the opponents in the northern quarter-final of the "Micky Mouse" Cup that some still referred to. But nobody laughed late that night; and it was late. It was a tense match, a goal for each side across normal time - Crewe's from Mathias Pogba on the stroke of half-time, with Rovers returning the favour with an equaliser in the 90th minute. That was from the penalty spot following a clumsy challenge by Matt Tootle that earned him a red card. A few Alex fans had already snuck out hoping to get an early night. They missed the extra time, although few chances were created as the teams became cagey and fearful of defeat. So the tie was concluded with penalties. Rovers fluffed their lines, but Lauri Dalla Valle, Harry Davis, Abdul Osman, Gregor Robertson and substitute Byron Moore did the business for Crewe. Suddenly the remaining mockers were silenced; the Alex had progressed to the northern semi-final. More silverware was glistening on the horizon.

I would not say that the JPT "run" transformed the season, as we slipped out of the FA Cup in the second round against League Two Burton Albion. But the league performances were consistent; and a key factor was home form. During November and December, Davis watched the fans celebrate fine wins over Colchester, Crawley, Bury and Carlisle in the league. The manager even signed a new rolling 18-month contract, putting supporters at ease after speculation had linked the Crewe boss with several other teams. Settling into League One was not a problem. The gaffer was content, and we all looked up longingly at the League One play-off places. That was asking too much, but the ongoing participation in the lower league cup was boosting confidence and proving to be a wonderful appendage to the season.

The northern semi-final saw Crewe once again back to winning ways at Gresty Road. Bradford City's form going into the game was patchy, to say the least. The Bantams boasted just two wins in nine, although one had been over Aston Villa in the first leg of the Carling Cup semi-final. The Yorkshire side was having an amazing cup run. That was a significant factor; their progression to the final of the more "senior" tournament hinged on defending a 3-1 lead away at Villa Park a week after the JPT match against Crewe. It would be harsh to suggest that some of their players' minds wandered, or that Bradford manager Phil Parkinson told his lads to hold back. Whatever, hopes that the Alex would at least make it to the area final proved justified, and a 4-1 scoreline was the outcome. The visitors took the lead, but an own goal leveller was followed by a clever Max Clayton header mid-way through the second half to settle our nerves. The Alex pressure mounted, and Bradden Inman and Chuks Aneke finished the job late into the game to give a somewhat distorted final score. Few of the near 3,000 crowd were bothered. We had a northern area final to contemplate, and it was only ten days away.

When Coventry were confirmed as our opponents (they beat Preston in their semi-final) there was a collective sigh. Our history against the Sky Blues wasn't bad, just not terribly consistent. I suppose it was the big-club syndrome, with little Crewe fearing the worst. In fact, the record across the previous decade was fairly balanced, although most of the encounters had been back in the Championship days. Most fans who enjoyed that era will recall Lee "Mr Popular" Hughes grabbing a hat-trick when Coventry beat us at Gresty Road in 2002. And then a comprehensive FA Cup defeat in January 2005 was a very forgettable experience. But May 2005, oh that sweet end-of-season finale that saw us survive on the last day. Goals from Michael Higdon and Steve Jones nullified former Alex frontman Dele Adebola's strike. He briefly threatened to send us down. So the JPT was our chance to gain the upper hand.

The first leg got Coventry fans all aflutter. The Internet message boards were dominated by their supporters, thousands suddenly coming out of the woodwork with a cup final in sight. It was their first chance to visit Wembley in years (their last saw them famously beat Tottenham 3-2 in the 1987 FA Cup final), and they turned out in numbers hoping to roar the Sky Blues on to success. In fact, the crowd of 31,054 was the highest attendance recorded for a JPT match outside of the final.

The arrogance, however, was staggering. Because of their numerical dominance, the Coventry fans saw the two-leg decider against Crewe as a foregone conclusion. They started booking trains and hotels in London before we'd kicked off the first game at the Ricoh Arena. They mocked and taunted pre-match, full of bravado and incredulous that so many Alex supporters had bothered making the trip. We actually took around 2,000 on Wednesday 20th February. It was a fabulous turn-out, but it was a tiny pocket of red amidst thousands of blues in the vast new stadium that Coventry were still calling home (at the time, a rent dispute was brewing and the Sky Blues' days at the Ricoh were numbered).

And so to the football... we have all been to dramatic games, where tackles, goals and off-the-ball incidents stick in the mind for years. Sometimes it's a lucky, against-the-odds result (Blackburn Rovers 0 Crewe 1, March 2000), or maybe a crazy scoreline (Barnet 4 Crewe 7, August 1991). Occasionally, it's because the result leaves everyone shocked (Crewe 1 Coventry 6, February 2002).

That night every Alex player delivered, from outstanding goalkeeping, resolute defending and hard-working midfield industry, to audacious and clinical forward play. Davis was forced to make changes before the match, but those who stepped up didn't let him or the travelling fans down.

A scoreless first half was the only real surprise, and that was largely down to some spectacular saves by Steve Phillips. Soon after the break, on-loan Bradden Inman lashed the first of two stunning strikes into the Coventry net. He converted his second with twelve minutes remaining and the vast crowd fell silent. It is one of the quirks of football; so many bodies packed into a stadium with just a pocket of supporters making all of the noise. It can be eerie, but the Alex contingent certainly made themselves heard. There was celebration, old songs and a few provocative taunts for good measure. To the right and left Coventry fans lashed out, pointing and gesticulating to singled-out Crewe lads. Nobody cared, especially when AJ Leitch-Smith sent the visitors into raptures and the locals scuttling home. He tucked the third Alex goal into the bottom corner and Davis and Baker punched the air. Chuks Aneke almost added a fourth, but that would have been greedy.

It was an impressive lead to take back to Gresty Road. The bookmakers didn't write them off, although Coventry's fortunes took a turn for the worse leading up to the game. It looked increasingly likely that their landlord would turf them out of the Ricoh Arena. Still, when we took our usual spot up in block "B" of the main stand for the second leg there was a little apprehension. It didn't help that a few Coventry fans had got tickets nearby. They chatted away with confidence, convinced that an early goal would be enough to spur their side on to an unlikely comeback and aggregate win. No way, we thought, even the Alex couldn't concede four goals at home. Could they?

A whopping 8,325 crowd made for a feisty atmosphere, with 2,300 from the Midlands rammed into the Popside and Railway End. Others were scattered around the main stand, some of them cocky enough to shout out as Sky Blue songs filled the air. They were up for it, and three early chances for the visitors lifted Coventry and put the Alex on the back foot. It wasn't a rearguard action, far from it. But City pressed and Steve Phillips was called upon several times before the break. Crewe lacked sparkle and the forward line that tormented away at the Ricoh looked timid and scared to run at the Coventry defenders. And yet we still led the tie by three clear goals.

The second half was relentless. James Bailey, Leon Clarke and Carl Baker kept Coventry's high-tempo game plan alive but still couldn't break through. Then the power shifted. Luke Murphy took control and delivered passes good enough for Inman, Leitch-Smith and Aneke to go close. We looked to have secured a penalty, but referee Graham Scott waved hopeful Alex players away. Then it could, and really should, have been wrapped up by Inman as the match official was contemplating stoppage time. The effort was smothered and the assistant indicated an unbelievable five additional minutes! There had been no goals, and just four bookings had given the referee cause to pause the action. So quite where that time came from baffled us all and spurred the visitors on further.

OWN GOAL!

The breakthrough came courtesy of Mark Ellis, but the Alex stopper was at the wrong end when he scored. His looping header over the stranded Phillips gave Coventry the slimmest lifeline. It was now one-nil on the night; crucially, it was three-one to Crewe overall.

Surely they could not fight back, could they? We were biting fingers not nails by now. The only source of amusement was watching Sky Blue fans walking away down Gresty Road from our lofty vantage point. Many dashed back as they heard the celebrations, but they were blocked by police and stewards.

Within seconds they were practically beating the doors down. Leon Clarke bulldozed past Ellis and Dugdale to head home from close range.

Time to panic: three-two on aggregate; the stuff of nightmares. No way, it couldn't happen! But still they came. One final push, a free-kick pumped deep into the Crewe area. It was mayhem. There were bodies everywhere; pushing, grabbing, every one of them desperate to make a connection. The coolest head belonged to Kelvin Mellor. He cleared and the referee's whistle allowed us all to breathe.

***

A few days after the incredible high of last-minute drama vs Coventry, it was once again time to queue for Wembley tickets. Our opponents were Southend. Stood there, in roughly the same spot we had nearly a year earlier for the play-off final, Ray and I had a mini confessional. It was the kind of thing you shouldn't admit to another supporter, but we know each other too well. I could sense that he wanted to get something off his chest, just as I did. Fans of clubs that have never made it to "new"

Wembley would shudder, but neither of us felt overly excited about the JPT final. There, I said it. It just didn't feel the same.

But much like the promotion the previous May, we felt that beating Southend was a foregone conclusion. There was something about the cup campaign that mirrored the swagger we had enjoyed during the unbeaten run during Davis' first season. It was unfounded, as our league form either side of the cup competition had been erratic. In the months leading up to the April final, we'd beaten MK Dons, Preston and Colchester, lost to Crawley, Portsmouth and Hartlepool, and drawn far too many matches to ever threaten the top seven promotion candidates. Still, this was a season of consolidation and realignment after the departure of two hugely influential players. The JPT was a lovely bonus. It just didn't feel particularly special. As a supporter who has been lucky to enjoy some wondrous days out at the national stadium, I still feel guilty about that.

Unlike the play-off day, I joined the Fordy coaches. I ditched the kids (and wife) in favour of a beery day out. To be honest, they weren't that bothered. In fact the Chelsea-supporting lads didn't know we'd reached the final. So I planned for a wholly different experience for my second trip to the hallowed turf.

This time, we parked up at a pub close to Wembley Way. The coaches somehow squeezed into the modest car park, row upon row manoeuvring into position until they were packed in like sardines. I'd say that we hit the beers soon after, but there was no chance. It wasn't the Green Man, no vast patio or garden area to spread out. With five and six deep at the bar it was a good twenty minutes before we sampled the first lager of the day. Then we talked, met with old mates once again and considered our drinking options. It had a proper away-day feel about it. There was more football chat as we had already lived that big day out nearly twelve months earlier. This was business. This was about winning a cup. There was nothing touristy about our jolly to London that day.

So let's get down to the main course. The Alex prepared thoroughly once again and utilised the excellent facilities at Arsenal's training ground, just as they did leading up to the play-off final. And whether you admire the Crewe manager or still harbour doubts, one thing that you cannot fault is his preparation ahead of crucial games. He gets the squad into peak condition - mentally and physically. When we got into Wembley, our players were running through early drills with the fitness coaches. The Southend lads were strolling about, snapping photos and waving to their considerable mass of supporters. They looked as though they were on holiday.

The crowd was 43,842 and the majority had travelled up from Southend for the day. Some estimates suggested that the Shrimpers brought over 30,000 fans from Kent. But that didn't matter. Interestingly, the biggest turnout for a final was recorded in 1988 - and it involved Steve Davis! The former Alex defender completed a move from Crewe to Turf Moor in October 1987, and inside six months he stepped out at the national stadium in front of 80,000 when his Burnley side lost 2-0 to Wolves in the Sherpa Van Trophy showpiece.

The most bizarre part of the pre-match build-up was realising that former Southend gaffer Paul Sturrock was sitting with the fans up in the stands. He'd been sacked in March having already secured the Wembley day out, the club's first final at the national stadium. New manager Phil Brown had the pleasure of leading the team out; only his third match in charge. He was yet to win a game since taking over!

And then it started, two teams marching proudly to the centre-circle. Those moments before kick-off were a sight to behold. The pyrotechnics dazzled and smoke filled the air. Balloons and clappers replaced the horns and ticker-tape of old, and the venue's speakers made the ground shake once again.

KICK-OFF!

There was significant action from the start, both sides creating openings, but the Alex pushed deep into Southend territory way before they could get into gear. And before many fans had taken their seats, Byron Moore picked up the ball after five minutes and prepared to take a corner kick.

What happened next was sublime, and was similar to Nick Powell's famous strike for ingenuity and execution. The build-up differed, but several players were involved. The muscle of Abdul Osman and Mark Ellis caused a commotion in the Southend area. They pushed and shoved, dragging defenders with them. Everyone expected a high ball for the Alex defenders to attack. Even Harry Davis stepped forward as Moore prepared to take the kick. But there was no run-up as he stroked the ball at forty-five degrees towards the edge of the box.

Southend panicked. They knew something was about to happen, but their reaction was in slow motion. Davis let the ball pass through his legs. But he had not been nut-megged. This had been carefully rehearsed on the training ground. It drew two defenders and allowed space to open up. Luke Murphy filled that void, arriving like a train from nowhere. He despatched a delightful shot with the inside of his boot wrapped lovingly around the ball.

It rose, curled and looped over the goalkeeper who could only watch on. The man on the back post was a spectator.

GOAL!

This time I went crazy. With no family to consider it was like any other road trip; beers and banter fusing as emotions exploded with football buddies. A huddle of bodies celebrated another incredible Wembley strike that would live long in the memory. And it could not have been timed better. We suddenly realised that we needed to settle.

As the stadium clock ticked on to 3:06pm the Crewe end began to clap again. It was a pre-arranged moment, a nod of appreciation, respect and condolence to defender Adam Dugdale. He and his partner, Nicola, tragically lost their baby son Jude a month earlier in March. The infant was just a few days old. The player was heartbroken, and was never likely to feature in the showpiece final that he helped to secure. Before that, Duggy only missed one game of the JPT run; the first round at Shrewsbury. Even attending the final was too much, so the Alex support chose to celebrate his shirt (number six) to let him know that we had him in our thoughts.

The ripple of applause soon grew as everyone realised that the time had arrived. The mark of respect had been well orchestrated via a #doitforduggy campaign on social media site Twitter. The Southend fans also clapped, in fact the whole stadium joined in. I was caught up in the moment, as were thousands of others. I am sure that I saw a few of the Alex players also clap along for a few seconds. There were tears, and for a minute the madness of football was forgotten.

In many ways the JPT played out much like our victory over Cheltenham a year earlier. We grabbed the initiative, and then Southend hit back. They just couldn't score. The Alex goal was blessed. Even the referee seemed to side with Crewe, dismissing penalty claims, ruling Shrimpers players offside and awarding us corners when the ball had clearly cannoned off a man in red. It was a refreshing change to have a few decisions go our way.

Southend headed over the bar, shot from range and tried to pick their way past Alex defenders - but all to no avail. Livewire striker Britt Assombalonga in particular had a bad day at the office, not once getting past Ellis properly. The Alex defender used every trick in the book to keep him away from goal. It was enough, and the half-time whistle was welcome respite from a sustained barrage from the team in blue.

That spectacular colour splashed across Wembley is something that I'll never forget. Perhaps it was the sheer volume of Southend supporters, massed ranks opposite us that made the stadium look full from our perspective. The crowd was nearly double the attendance that had watched us win the play-off final. It was incredible. To our right was all red, although the left-hand blocks beyond the Alex fans were empty. That didn't matter. We were underdogs in the stands but titans out on the pitch. It was still a close encounter, but I didn't see any apprehensive faces as the players came back out after the interval.

The second half was a proper end-to-end cup tie, but only after the Alex stirred the opposition into action. Clayton did the damage, slotting home a drag-back from the unselfish Moore.

TWO-NIL!

That still wasn't game over, as Southend really came at us. They had a goal disallowed, Davis headed off the line, and then Matt Tootle did similar but with his boot. And then we countered. AJ Leitch-Smith was desperately unlucky, seeing a shot well saved and then denied by the crossbar. Their goalkeeper performed heroics to keep others off the scoresheet, but his team mates couldn't drag themselves back into contention with a goal. Once again it was our day. The Southend lads kept going, but only until the referee made it official. There was only ever going to be one winner.

Murphy took the cheers as he staggered up those daunting Wembley steps, and then hoisted the huge trophy above his head. Over 10,000 cheered, but the noise wasn't quite the same as when Dave Artell confirmed our promotion from League Two with a firm grip around the play-off trophy. There was a more subdued euphoria, almost respectful. I think that was in part because many realised that it was, after all, just a game of football. Nearly two hours earlier we had applauded and chanted the name of a man who should have been at Wembley with us, battling away at the heart of the Alex defence.

Later, captain for the day Luke Murphy summed it up when he spoke to *The Crewe Chronicle*: 'That effort from all the lads was for Duggy. He should've been here, he's a massive character. Nobody should have to go through what he has, but I want him to know that all the lads have been thinking about him.'

THEY DID IT FOR DUGGY!

Travelling back I felt pretty smug. The Alex stock was soaring. They were spoiling us. Back-to-back Wembley visits, a half-decent league campaign and a team brimming with youthful talent. We were the darlings of the English game. If I'm honest, lifting that JPT silverware still didn't feel special, nowhere near as satisfying as the promotion achieved twelve months earlier. If anything, I enjoyed the sheer drama of the area final second leg more, when Coventry pushed us so close in the dying minutes of the match. But it was growing on me. And I shouldn't be so ungrateful.

Others on the coach were animated. They were giddy with success. I just felt sated, that after dinner feeling when you have eaten too much. I had feasted and become greedy. The pudding had tipped me over the edge. There was only one way I'd rediscover my mojo; that meant drinking and dancing the night away with like-minded football fools.

***

Eleven months earlier, the play-off final journey ended for yours truly when the coach pulled into Crewe. The kids were knackered and Mrs H wasn't over keen on extending an already very long day. So I didn't enjoy the celebrations back at the club. I saw pictures and stories posted online by others. I regretted it for weeks, although the family had to come first.

The JPT jolly was wholly different. There was no way I was missing out on the post-Wembley celebrations that so many had described to me a year earlier. I even retained enough battery charge to ensure that video could be captured to complete a montage I'd put together to sum up the day. But a good hour of drinking ensured that wobbly hands and hazy eyes made the final clips of my film rather shaky. That didn't matter. I lost myself in fabulous recollections with friends, jokes about the unstoppable Alex bandwagon and the high hopes for the future. It was tremendous, all washed down with too many lagers as we awaited the arrival of the official coach.

A sign of the club's togetherness came with the trophy itself. I held a position by the double doors that lead into the main suite. We all expected man-of-the-moment Luke Murphy to be carrying the JPT silverware, at least that's what I and most others thought. Instead it was a man who was cruelly ruled out of the final through injury. Mathias Pogba emerged from the calm of the corridor into the mayhem of red, white, beers and camera flashes. The lighting was low, but disco beams gave it a surreal nightclub feel as the temperature soared. The room rocked and the players snaked in to the madness, a single line of footballers genuinely taken aback by the scene that greeted them.

The Alex manager almost disappeared under a scramble of photo-takers, autograph-hunters and hand-shakers. He greeted them all. He had time for every one of them. In the background Neil Baker was in full flow. He started the chant and the crowd provided the deafening chorus. "He's Abdul, he's Abdul, he's Abdul f******g Osman" sang Crewe's assistant and about three hundred delirious others. He loved every second and the whole room bounced along to his words.

There was a moment of quieter reflection when compère Andy Scoffin called for everyone to remember those not present: Dario Gradi (poorly), Adam Dugdale (grieving) and former kit man John Fleet (sadly passed). There was a respectful cheer, fitting for the raucous football occasion.

Then John Bowler walked across the dance floor as Davis and Bakes continued to entertain the crowd. He cut a lonely figure. That probably sounds daft, but the attention was all on the management duo and the players that mingled with the jubilant crowd. I wandered over and shook his hand. He smiled, genuinely shocked by the commotion all around. We only swapped a few words, but I wanted him to share the spoils of that incredible success. He contributed to the resurgence as much if not more than others. He made those tough decisions, had faith in promoting from within (again) when other chairmen might have panicked. In the background he supported Gradi all along, because he was a patient, loyal and ultimately very wise man. And then he trusted in Davis.

It was a close-run thing eighteen months earlier, when relegation was a real concern, but now it was time to celebrate. This was his reward for endless hours of soul searching and worry, time invested in Crewe Alexandra for the good of the club. He walked away to acknowledge others, past younger fans who had no idea who he was. He's a great man; perhaps the best chairman in the Football League.

HISTORY MAN

The tail-end of the 2012/13 season felt like the morning after the night before. The buzz of JPT success at Wembley lasted just three days. The trophy was still doing the rounds back in Crewe when the team headed down to London to take on Brentford in the league. There were still six fixtures to fulfil; there was no time to relax. But Steve Davis watched on as his side was comfortably beaten at Griffin Park. I wouldn't say that the players were suffering a post-final hangover, as the Bees were a tidy unit with credible promotion aspirations. They despatched the Alex 2-0 to ease themselves into a play-off position.

The following three games didn't set alarm bells ringing, although a trio of defeats did rather take the shine off the early-April glory at the national stadium. Thankfully the teams that relieved us of points were all still chasing promotion; so it was no disgrace.

Doncaster edged a decent game at Gresty Road 2-1 when the Alex had been winning (Rovers would ultimately top the division); Swindon ran amok with a timely 4-1 win that propelled them into the play-off positions; and then Yeovil took a first minute lead at Huish Park and never looked likely to concede. They would enjoy promotion as runners-up. So although the season looked set to end on a downer, the results looked much worse on paper than they actually were.

Thankfully, we didn't need points when Sheffield United came to Crewe for the penultimate game of the campaign. The Alex won courtesy of a Chuks Aneke goal just after the break. That took us above the sixty point mark and capped a solid nine months of consolidation. It left just Walsall, visitors to Gresty Road on the final day of the season. The fixture would prove more significant than anyone could possibly have imagined.

An interview with Graham McGarry set tongues wagging. The Radio Stoke man was chatting with the Alex gaffer about the ongoing success, coping with player sales and what the future held. It became apparent that Davis had a surprise up his sleeve. Although he couldn't confirm it until the final day, there was a good chance we'd be treated to a home-grown XI stepping out on the pitch at the same time.

The idea had been discussed for donkeys' years, ever since Crewe Alexandra and Dario Gradi nailed the club colours to the mast and committed to a youth-driven future. Davis reiterated what had been said many times before, that he was determined to invest in, develop and prosper alongside the club's young players. The concept went hand-in-hand with Gradi's philosophy. He was, after all, the man who arrived with a plan, to nurture footballers capable of executing *The Beautiful Game* with aplomb. For various reasons, a senior side made up of academy products never happened during his watch.

For starters, a large part of Gradi's tenure was spent in "The Championship" (the second tier). Throwing eleven young men into action at that level against, largely speaking, former Premier League players would have been like tossing lambs to lions. Not necessarily because of a gulf in class, but the nous that comes with three, four and five years of top-flight competition cannot be underestimated. Drop down to the kick-and-rush of some Sunday League football and it's the same there. Sixteen and seventeen year old lads who stand out at school can't cope with overweight forty-somethings. It's not pace, skill or desire; it's knowing where to stand, how to commit subtle fouls without the referee noticing, and second-guessing your opponent. Even the most talented young players need time to understand such "gamesmanship" and how to deal with football's underbelly of dirty tricks.

Perhaps the closest that Gradi came was with the players that emerged as the class of '97. Promotion to the second level of English football had just been secured for the first time in Crewe Alexandra's history. Instead of dashing out to buy experience and mortgage the club's future with extortionate wages, Gradi trusted in kids. A certain Sir Alex Ferguson was doing similar at Old Trafford around the same time. While the redoubtable Scot had David Beckham, Paul Scholes and Nicky Butt, Gradi put faith in Kenny Lunt, Seth Johnson, Gareth Whalley, Dele Adebola, Kevin Street, Mark Rivers and Steve Garvey.

It wasn't quite a baptism of fire, as several of the players who figured in Crewe's first match at the higher lever had considerable experience already. But this was a whole new ball game. Many of the opponents were from cities not provincial towns, with ex-Premiership stars scattered across daunting line-ups that suddenly looked bigger, stronger and faster than anything the Gradi graduates had ever encountered. The young Crewe lads had to grow up fast.

Away at Swindon on the opening day of that 1997/98 season the Alex coped, but never looked like winning the game. A few contentious refereeing decisions went against us, and we eventually lost 2-0 on a blistering hot August afternoon. We all applauded the effort, and few had concerns about our ability to survive in the division.

And it was the most exceptional season, with victories over Portsmouth, Norwich, Sheffield United, Manchester City and both Potteries rivals, Stoke and Port Vale. The away-days were dazzling, full-on city stops instead of worn out towns with tumbleweed blowing down the high street. Quite what those other clubs thought about Crewe is another matter; but they acknowledged our desire to play football and applauded our home-grown talent. It was the stuff of schoolboy dreams, and our schoolboys excelled.

One game at Gresty Road, however, stood out because of a post-match conversation. Sunderland beat the Alex by three goals to nil in December 1997. The Crewe players were brimming with confidence with some fantastic results already recorded, but they couldn't contain Peter Reid's Black Cats. Kevin Phillips scored after two minutes to set the tone and unsettle the Alex. Nicky Summerbee doubled the lead before the interval; and then Irish international Niall Quinn grabbed the third to finish us off late in the game. In reality, it could have been ten.

Post-match beers were enjoyed in the Alex Suite in those days; the bar behind the Pop Side stand. Players from both teams drifted through after they had showered, and most were happy to chat with supporters. Quinn was forthright in his assessment of Gradi's team. It was 'men against boys' he told us over a pint of lager. He was very dismissive, adamant that the team needed to adapt quickly if we wanted to prosper at that level. And he was right. That's exactly how the match appeared from the sidelines. Sunderland were not a particularly dirty side, but they used strength and guile to shunt us off the ball and disrupt our flow. It was a harsh lesson for the academy lads, one that sadly confirmed that pure football would not always win the day.

Different styles suit different teams. With almost exactly the same matchday squad, the Alex beat Manchester City 1-0 on Boxing Day. Not only did Gradi's players stand up to some of the game's biggest names, they stood out and fully deserved to win. I'm convinced that such victories that season convinced the wider football community that Crewe Alexandra's methods and its players needed to be taken seriously.

It didn't always work out immediately, and some players were thrown into the fire too soon. One example that sticks in my mind involves midfielder David Vaughan. It was the opening weeks of the 2000/01 season, Crewe's fourth year in the higher division. First up at Gresty Road: Blackburn; the classic former Premiership club, accustomed to the big time and littered with highly-paid stars. Their line-up that day included Gary Flitcroft, Damien Duff, Jason McAteer, David Dunn and Nathan Blake. They packed more than a punch. The Alex had made minor adjustments to the playing staff that had finished 19th the previous season, but the matchday squad to face Rovers still contained seven academy players. Vaughan was just seventeen years old. From high up in the main stand he looked like a schoolboy. He was a slight and compact player, just five feet and five inches tall, and against the internationals in blue and white halves he looked out of his depth. He looked like a startled rabbit when the ball came near him, and he was substituted at half time. It was Vaughan's only appearance of the season.

Thankfully, the staff at Reaseheath kept working with him and the player obviously had the mettle to continue. He was back the next season and clocked up sixteen appearances in league and cup games. He even played against Everton in the exciting fifth round FA Cup encounter that saw the Alex narrowly edged out after a replay. Vaughan was introduced slowly but surely. It was testament to the player, Gradi and the other coaches, that he went on to complete over six full seasons at Gresty Road. Moreover, he excelled in the Premier League with Blackpool and Sunderland, enjoyed a season in Spain with Sociedad, and represented Wales. Not bad for a young lad that once looked out of his depth at Gresty Road!

CONVEYOR BELT.

A few years later the likes of Ben Rix, Dean Ashton, Stephen Foster, David Wright, Lee Bell and Rob Hulse were all permanent fixtures in the senior side. It was what most observers called the Crewe "conveyor belt" of talent. They all prospered in the Championship, as did Gary Roberts, Michael Higdon, Billy Jones, Michael O'Connor and Nicky Maynard towards the end of Gradi's time as manager (pre-Steve Holland). The list goes on and on. Each and every season there was five, six or seven "local" lads in the team.

So why didn't Gradi do it, take the plunge and play a home-grown XI? Was it a lack of conviction, fear of failure or the simple fact that he never had all positions covered at the same time? As a supporter I wanted it to happen, and I cannot believe that Gradi didn't want to stand in the technical area, proud as punch, watching a team entirely of his own making kick-off a competitive match. He must have observed countless games in training, reserve team friendlies and U21 fixtures when his players stood up to the test. So it must have been timing, circumstance and availability of certain players that held him back.

The only other consideration would be whether his selection might affect teams in promotion or relegation positions. This happened at the end of 1997/98 and also 2002/03. On both occasions, although the Alex had already reached safety, their opponents were involved in the play-off positions. Would putting out a team of eighteen to twenty-three-year-olds be considered unprofessional? Some might see it as a weakened side destined to lose, and therefore likely to distort the final standings in the league table? Personally, I have never accepted that. It goes on during the core season, when managers choose to "rest" key players ahead of a cup tie or crucial league match. And why shouldn't a manager be entitled to utilise squad players, get them match fit and generate real competition for all places? As long as those selected come from the squad registered at the beginning of the season, or in line with league rules – why not?

There were end-of-season opportunities, even during the Championship days. In the final week of the 2000/01 and 2003/04 seasons the Alex were home and dry, not dependent upon the last result. I'd side with the latter as the best opportunity to have made history, if Gradi had wanted to go for it. Against Norwich City there was a chance; the visitors had already been confirmed as champions. It was an end-of-season party for their fans, and they packed Gresty Road and invaded the pitch after their 3-1 victory. The daft thing is, Gradi was so close to achieving the dream. Eight home-grown players featured that day (David Wright, Chris McCready, Stephen Foster, David Vaughan, Kenny Lunt, Neil Sorvel and Dean Ashton, plus Michael Higdon on the substitutes' bench). Even Craig Hignett was part of the matchday squad, although technically he was developed at Liverpool and then made his professional debut with the Alex when he was eighteen years old). In the background, Billy Jones and Richard Walker had featured that season but were unavailable. So it was possible, but the moment passed.

For Gradi there was always one position that caused more issues than most. The midfield was prolific, with new talent emerging every season. Up front there was also a steady supply of goalscorers. The defence took longer to flourish, but eventually a stream of academy lads were preferred to bought-in stoppers. Crewe always struggled finding a goalkeeper.

For many years it was Mark Gayle and Mark Smith, and then the ever-popular "Aussie 'keeper" Jason Kearton. Around the 2003/04 season, three men dominated between the sticks: Clayton Ince, Ben Williams and Ade Bankole. They came from far and wide, but never Crewe. And yet there was a young lad called Stuart Tomlinson bubbling under the surface. I had to check, but he DID play that season, away at West Ham United in the league. Ince was injured in the 86th minute when the Alex already trailed 4-2. It was only a few minutes, but he was there, available and capable. Why didn't Gradi take a chance on the young fella in that final match against Norwich, even for the last few minutes? My only conclusion is that the fear of his side taking an embarrassing beating against rampant Norwich deterred Gradi. That could have ruined player confidence. That could have set his plans back.

JUST GO FOR IT!

So fielding a team of home-grown kids was always going to be a challenge. It would take a brave man to pull it off. Davis obviously had the balls to go for it. With promotion secured in his first six months, and the Johnstone's Paint Trophy still gleaming on the Alex mantelpiece after a decent season of consolidation, the new man was determined to deliver another surprise for fans still dizzy by the recent transformation.

For Davis, taking the decision to play eleven academy products was not a crazy leap of faith. The 2012/13 season had been played out using many of the club's young players. It had been a matter of necessity, not an order from above. Gradi was now heading up the academy operation of course, with daily dialogue with the manager ongoing. And yet the team belonged to Davis. He was moulding a new style, a way of playing that was sympathetic to Gradi's core principles, but ever demanding of success and positive results.

Crucially, Walsall had nothing to play for. The result would have no effect on the key ups and downs, no real bearing on the final league table. In many ways it was the kind of opportunity that rarely arises, when other clubs could not point an accusing finger. End-of-season games nearly always carry some weight, and creating bad feeling with other clubs reliant on other results is never a good idea. Grudges fester and can cause problems in the future, on many fronts.

The main consideration was the goalkeeping position. Here, perhaps, was Davis' greatest dilemma. The season had seen three goalkeepers used: the vastly experienced Steve Phillips, and Alan Martin. Youth player Ben Garratt had no senior appearances to his name - not even a brief run-out as a late substitute, although he had warmed the bench in the early phase of the season. He had celebrated his eighteenth birthday two days before the Walsall fixture. He was what most observers might call "green" and untested. And yet there was undoubted potential, something that had earned him a number of starts with the England U17, U18 and U19 teams, sometimes alongside Nick Powell and Max Clayton. If ever Davis wanted to take a chance on a goalkeeper it was now.

***

There was a fabulous anticipation ahead of the match. It was a beautiful day, a little windy but glorious sunshine as always making the end-of-season swansong an occasion to remember. With nothing to play for, everyone was in party mood. The Walsall fans had travelled the short distance in numbers, and they also seemed excited by the prospect of a history-making game. The news had spread far and wide. Any rivalries were put aside, and there was genuine interest in what might be achieved.

So the tension mounted as the second and third pints went down during heated conversations in the Corner Bar; and it was all great debate. Would Garratt get the nod in goal? Would Davis start with the kids or make up the eleven with a couple of late substitutes?

One of the best questions asked if all of our players qualified as academy graduates! Indeed, players like Adam Dugdale had come, gone and returned to the fold, and Kelvin Mellor moved to Crewe from Nantwich Town when he was sixteen. Only a few of them could tell dreamy tales of starting out as six-year-olds at the old Soccer Centre near Shavington. But at 16, 17 and 18 years of age they had all been coached at Reaseheath. Crucially, the lads likely to be involved had all completed the necessary scholarship and "graduated" from the academy. So it was genuine. We just needed to see the evidence in black and white on the team sheet before we started to celebrate the landmark.

The waiting ended just after 2:00pm when the first updates trickled onto the Internet. Multiple mobile handsets delivered the team news. Even the Saddlers fans huddled around, desperate to see if the Crewe manager had taken the plunge. He had, and as we picked down the list of names everyone grinned. It was about to happen. We were proud. Our club was breaking new ground.

The photo on the back cover of the book paints a better picture than words ever could. Young men, arms wrapped around shoulders, smiles and chests puffed out. It shows the starting XI, an ensemble of Crewe academy players captured before kick-off by photographer Pete Warburton (see later chapter).

For the record, here are the names of those players, including (in brackets) the number of first team appearances accumulated before the Walsall match. The statistics were checked, but please accept my apologies if any of the details are not 100% accurate.

BACK ROW, left to right: Ryan Colclough (21), Kelvin Mellor (59), George Ray (5), Ben Garratt (0), Harry Davis (76), Luke Murphy (139).

FRONT ROW, left to right: Byron Moore (247), AJ Leitch-Smith (97), Max Clayton (73), Matt Tootle (124), Ollie Turton (27).

Any suggestion that the team lacked quality, experience or match time was blown out of the water when the collective appearance statistic was analysed: 868 Alex games played between them. This was no naïve bunch of young lads; they had served their time and fully deserved to be on that pitch. In many ways it was not a gamble. During the season every one of them except Garratt had featured, many holding down a regular position. There had been a dress rehearsal of sorts, three weeks earlier in London. Nine of the players appeared at Wembley in the JPT final. And of course they trained together each day. The idea that the side had been plucked from kindergarten was laughable. Still, it was a fabulous achievement for them to start the match, and the English game looked on in envy. As the teams were announced and boomed out around the stadium, each name was cheered as though we were acknowledging testimonials. Even some of the Walsall fans joined in.

When the action began in earnest, it was a tight affair. At the core of the Alex side was Luke Murphy. Without him I wonder if the "youth" idea would have been progressed. He was central to almost everything that Crewe Alexandra achieved during 2012/13. Indeed, during Davis's second season in charge the talisman midfielder made 48 appearances. That, in part, was down to the business done in late August 2012, when fellow midfielder Ashley Westwood was sold to Aston Villa. That left Murphy to roam free; he was able to dominate the central playmaking position. If you get that sorted, pull the right strings and kick-start the best attacks, then every scout will drool. And they did. But you have to get it right. A few wrong moves, getting caught out of position or gifting possession to the opposition and you can also look a fool. Murphy had no intention of fluffing his lines. He was the leader of men; and they were young men with an average age of 21 years that played against Walsall.

As for the "kids" not being able to cope against the old hands from the West Midlands, the first half performance left none of the 6,547 crowd in any doubt. The Saddlers attacked quickly and tried several direct manoeuvres, perhaps assuming that an early goal would shatter their opponents' confidence. What they discovered was a wall of determination. When George Ray slipped he was bailed out by Garratt who must have played out multiple scenarios in the days leading up to matchday. His debut was not going to be spoiled. He didn't disappoint, and grew in confidence throughout the ninety minutes. And Ray also dusted himself down and continued to stroke the ball out of defence to the waiting Murphy. There was no panic. They all knew the drill. It was a million training sessions played out for real.

At half-time it was still goal-less, and it was a balanced game. The Saddlers looked competent and well-organised, but they couldn't score. Up front for Crewe both Clayton and Leitch-Smith had run like demons, but to no effect. So the academy reunion was eventually broken up as the manager went for the jugular. And Crewe had to win. Anyone could pitch a "weakened" side and laugh it off later when the team lost or limped home with a draw. But this was a statement of intent. The message had to be clear: Crewe Alexandra can play an academy side that is good enough to compete in League One. For forty five minutes they had done their job. Now they needed a boost. As fans, we couldn't complain. We had seen the cream of the Reaseheath crop, but the ruthless streak evident in the management team extended to the Crewe support. We all wanted the points. Ending the season on a high was now of paramount importance.

So Davis swapped Clayton (for Chuks Aneke) and Leitch-Smith (for Bradden Inman), both on sixty four minutes. Looking back, both men were on loan at Crewe, so the move sent out a strong signal that the players were wanted here at Gresty Road. They complemented the academy kids. They were part of the manager's plans. It would prove to be a cunning bit of psychology.

The tactical switch paid immediate dividends. The Alex started to dominate. The substitutes had done what the manager always asked of his players; they had analysed the game, watched for the gaps and weaknesses. They made an impact, freeing up space, stretching the visitors and forcing errors. But when the opening goal came it was fitting that it was made in Crewe. Moore (the oldest Alex player on the pitch at just 24 years of age) skipped past a defender and surged into the box.

The Walsall goalkeeper was drawn close and as the Crewe winger pushed the ball forward his legs were taken.

PENALTY!

Any one of five players could have taken the resultant spot kick, but there was only one man for the job: Captain Murphy. He stepped up on 78 minutes and made no mistake, tucking the ball past Sam Johnson in goal. That was his ninth of the season, a superb return from a midfielder who had probably created thirty more for his team mates.

Crewe's second was instigated by Colclough. The next-generation winger was too fast and tricky for his marker and fed a simple ball to Inman. He chose the team ahead of personal gain and set up Aneke. If any of the non-Alex boys deserved a goal it was him. From fifteen yards out he curled a delightful effort past the goalkeeper. The ball clattered off the underside of the bar for dramatic effort.

GAME OVER.

It was the perfect day, a solid win and a clean sheet. A few minutes for substitute Adam Dugdale would have lifted the roof; but supporters still applauded him as he warmed up on the touchline in the final minutes. The sun shone, the chairman beamed and the young players lapped the pitch to soak up the adulation being heaped upon them from an adoring home crowd. Even some of the Walsall fans stayed to watch. The academy lads paraded the Johnstone's Paint Trophy, passing it from one to another, as most of them had taken part at Wembley.

On the last day of the season they had capped it all by transporting what usually happened on the Reaseheath training pitches to a professional, competitive match. They were proud to have made history, and Gradi watched on delighted to have seen it happen and content that he had set the wheels in motion many years earlier.

'It's a little piece of history,' gushed Davis, speaking to BBC Sport after the match. 'It's the first time this club has ever played an entire team of academy lads.'

Although the manager was relatively new to the job, it was apparent how much the occasion meant to him. There was no self-importance; he was just incredibly proud of the club. 'Everybody plays their part through the academy from Dario downwards. They've worked hard on their development and I've just tried to carry it on over the last 18 months and instil a bit of belief in how good they are,' he added modestly, almost playing down his role in proceedings. In reality, he had taken the boldest steps and made Gradi's dream come true.

The footnote to the fairytale story detailed above is a lesson in harsh economic reality, especially for a club like Crewe Alexandra. The history-making showpiece was the ultimate shop window. Scouts from clubs the length and breadth of the country had flocked to the main stand vantage point countless times during the season. Although Powell and Westwood had been snapped up twelve months earlier, everyone knew that many others were ripe for picking.

For all of the platitudes, with the club's finest eleven graduates on show at the same time, it was always likely that the Walsall match would be their last together. Moreover, it was another headache in the making for Davis who watched the season's finale with both pride and trepidation. He knew that the club had to balance its books, and the substantial investment at Reaseheath that had allowed the Alex to field that academy side needed funding. As supporters cheered another three points, the manager was planning for the 2013/14 season, when one or maybe two of the side would be gone.

Murphy was the main concern. How could Davis formulate anything without his anchor man? And yet the player deserved a move to bigger and (it pains me to say) better things. As an ambitious young footballer himself in the past, Davis knew there was no holding the lad back. That would have been wrong. It would have gone against the club's core promises. So we all knew that it would happen, and eventually it did. Murphy signed for Leeds United in July that summer. It was essential business for Crewe Alexandra and ensured that the club could be run largely debt-free for another few years.

Everyone wished Murphy good luck. He did much for the Crewe cause, and more than four seasons in the red shirt cannot be sniffed at. In his final season he was integral to most Alex moves. Few underestimated the impact his departure would have. In fact, when I grabbed a word with Davis during the following pre-season, he highlighted the sale of Murphy as THE factor that he (and Baker) knew would weight heaviest as the new campaign progressed. With Murphy gone, there was a void. They knew this, and they reacted knowing that things had to change. They did not have the personnel to play the passing game that had been so fluid across the previous eighteen months. And the sales seemed to be increasing. It was likely to get worse.

Davis was by now plugging holes and making running repairs on the hoof. But no bought-in players (on Crewe's budget) could offer the same creativity of the recently-departed playmaker. They would have to look elsewhere, to loans and short-term affordable purchases; at least until the next wave of academy stars emerged.

It was a bitter-sweet pill. The engine-room of the team had been ripped out. Gradi started the ball rolling and instilled a dream for the club to chase; to nurture, produce, play and sell on. He always wanted to see eleven of them in action together. Davis made it finally happen. Now he had to deal with the consequences of that success.

JUDAS

The title is harsh but it stuck with me following a discussion in the pub soon after the 2012/13 season had finished. The chat was about loyalty in football; the frantic turnover of managers, and of course how long Steve Davis would stay at the Alex. His stock was high. He'd achieved promotion from League Two, won the Johnstone's Paint Trophy and fielded a home-grown side in a professional match. Oh, and let's not forget setting the club's unbeaten record... all in eighteen months! The man was a hero to us, and the nation watched on with green eyes. He was a successful, loyal manager who had carried on the club's ethos. And because he was at Crewe Alexandra there was the unwritten rule that he had played good, honest passing football along the way. It was no surprise that he was attracting attention from the bigger clubs.

So after the historic end-of-season send-off against Walsall, in mid-May Davis blotted his copybook. He was linked to the vacant position at Wolverhampton Wanderers. Not only that, he followed up the interest and spoke to club officials in the Midlands. It was a shock to the system for Crewe fans, a real wake-up call. His achievements at the Alex had made him a target, as well as our academy players. The feedback from supporters was mixed, but many were unhappy that he could consider a move so soon.

The reaction from some was hostile because this was actually the third link to other clubs since Davis had taken over from Gradi. The first was tenuous, more gossip than bona fide contact, but it made many Crewe fans nervous. Media reports spoke of "whispers" and "rumoured approaches" in the weeks after our tremendous play-off success. Davis was linked with Birmingham City, and Internet fans were quick to register their displeasure. The papers carried details soon after, as there were no other football stories to fill their column inches.

With only seven months in the hotseat, we got an idea of how ambitious Davis was after he spoke to one of the area's newspapers. 'I've got no desire to leave Crewe or step up anywhere yet or anything like that. I'm here to develop and I want to continue that development here. But people who know me know I'm ambitious,' he told *The Staffordshire Evening Sentinel*. 'I want to manage at the highest level I possibly can. That won't go away, and I want to do it with this club,' he added. That was heartening, and gave fans belief that the gaffer was determined to achieve more with Crewe. Longer term, however, few dared guess what might happen. The Brummie story was put to bed when Lee Clark was appointed at St. Andrews in late June.

The speculation was something that everyone at Gresty Road would have to deal with on an increasing basis. If a job came up, someone would suggest Davis as the ideal fit. As supporters we have done it for years with players. A given striker would, if we could agree wages, be perfect for the Alex. When a midfielder was out-of-contract, hours would be spent pontificating about the pros and cons of his tackling abilities and ball distribution. Invariably, the clubs concerned had heard nothing official. But that's the nature of football chatter. We all love to deliberate and scheme, map out often impractical ideas that remain the stuff of dreams. With the shoe on the other foot, we hated hearing others covet OUR manager.

When the 2012/13 season began, the managerial merry-go-round went quiet. Clubs basked in the August and September sunshine, and chairmen the length and breadth of the country backed their managers to the hilt, even when the early results had been poor. Late summer and early autumn is football's honeymoon period. Wind the clock forward a few games, when perhaps fifteen matches have produced only a handful of points, and then clubs start to panic.

Big clubs were floundering in all divisions, and for some twitchy chairman it was already time to act. The Burnley situation was different. Manager Eddie Howe returned to Bournemouth leaving the Turf Moor club looking for a new man. The usual suspects were lined up as maybes, probables and favourites. Davis was in the frame. He had superb links with the club, having played there in the late 1980s and early 90s. And why wouldn't a Championship team look at Davis? When the Alex lifted the League Two play-off trophy the "rookie" manager had only lost four of his 32 games in charge. That was some record, the bulk amassed during the amazing unbeaten run through to Wembley. Throw in the hugely successful stint at his former club, Nantwich, and it all pointed to him being a winner.

When the rumours of the Turf Moor meet-up trickled into the public domain there was anxiety. Fans were concerned, surprised even, that the new man might depart (it was still less than one year since he had taken over from Gradi). And then it was anger because we could find ourselves without a manager.

Davis was on a short-list of ten candidates and sat down for an interview at a hotel on the edge of the Lancashire town. He later described the process as "a learning curve" and "testing the water" as he hadn't had to apply for a job since he left school. Amazingly, Davis had never attended a formal interview; never as a player, and his appointment at Nantwich had been casual. Onto Crewe there had been little need to sit down around the table. Everyone knew him, one of his lads was at the Alex academy, and the links between Crewe and Nantwich Town were strong. So he wanted to dip his toe in the water. That's what he told me a week after the event when we discussed another ongoing project. He never thought he'd get the Burnley job, and found the panel-style grilling an intimidating experience. But he did face questions and outline his vision for the Clarets' future. That was enough to concern any Crewe fan.

Around that time, I was working on the early years of Davis's biography. I trusted him, and although his answers were somewhat guarded when the interview situation was mentioned, I never doubted what he said. Burnley was a club close to his heart, but I think he knew that it was a move too soon. Compared to the Alex, the Turf Moor outfit boasted a huge fan base. They had Premier League aspirations and a little cash in the bank. Who wouldn't want to have a crack, especially an ambitious young manager who was on a roll?

'It's like anything in life; you have been given a compliment that someone else is supposedly interested in your services so you are doing something right,' Davis told *The Sentinel* as he tried to diffuse the situation. It didn't help matters that he was yet to sign a new contract at Gresty Road. That added to the intrigue. The new deal was on the table, bouncing between the manager, club and various solicitors. These things have to be done right, but fans started second-guessing what would unfold and why the process had been delayed. Many believed that the situation was more sinister than anyone would admit, especially when there was no official word from Crewe Alexandra.

A few days after the story surfaced, in the bar after we'd beaten Swindon 2-1, suspicious eyes followed the manager as he made his way to the club's offices. He wasn't uncomfortable with the attention, but it was apparent that he didn't want to discuss the matter, or add fuel to the fire. He is a private man, and he has never been one to hog the limelight. Now he just wanted to avoid the spotlights that were trying to track his next move.

The simple fact is that he was not and never will be Dario Gradi. The day that he accepted the Crewe managerial challenge, he was always going to be compared to the great man. That meant on the pitch, the style adopted by the team, the "fair play" of his players, and of course longevity. It was crazy to even consider it, but many fans assumed that Davis would be following directly in Gradi's footsteps - for the next thirty years.

Steve Holland faced a similar dilemma from the outset, and perhaps he was put under the microscope more so than Davis. Not only was Holland the former academy director at Crewe, but he had similar traits to Gradi. They even sounded the same on radio interviews!

Then there was the very "unique" Gudjon Thordarson. He was an aberration, but he would also have been measured against Gradi's many achievements had he remained at the club. Thankfully, he did not. He and we moved on, once again with Gradi in charge, but we craved a new man prepared to take us forward. For so many years we had known only stability. We had been spoiled by Gradi's commitment to us and the Alex.

The loyalty card is a big deal to football supporters. Despite countless kicks in the teeth, when players and managers arrive, we always hope that they will show undying devotion to "our" club. We want our cake and we want to eat it. It is an unrealistic, crazy and unfounded hope.

We never had such worries with Gradi. For those with short memories or anyone unaware of the details, he famously declined an approach from Portuguese club Benfica in the 1990s. He was committed to Crewe, and with each year and every success, he would set himself and the club fresh challenges. We crept up the leagues, the stadium was improved and the Reaseheath academy flourished. There was, however, always work to be done, and for Gradi it was/is a labour of love. He was still beavering away at Reaseheath while his successor was being interviewed at Turf Moor.

The Burnley situation was resolved when Sean Dyche got the nod, a man with a successful stint at Championship side Watford already under his belt. I'm not sure that Davis was genuinely in the running, as Burnley needed guarantees. He admitted that the interview was tough. Although he stood up to questioning well, he could only describe success in the bottom division. Burnley needed more. It was great practice for Davis and I suspect that the Lancashire club has kept his details on file; one for the future, perhaps? Back at Crewe we moved on. But we couldn't help looking over our shoulder for the next approach.

Davis always maintained that he still had much to achieve at Gresty Road. That involved winning a cup competition, which he went on to achieve some months after the Burnley kerfuffle died down. But by the summer of 2013, he had accomplished that and more. When his academy boys beat Walsall his CV was sprinkled with managerial fairy dust. So when the vacancy cropped up at Molineux after Dean Saunders was sacked, there was real apprehension.

Wolverhampton Wanderers was a wholly different scenario to anything that had gone before. On May 22nd, 2013, the BBC carried a story that suggested Davis was the frontrunner for the job. There was no concrete evidence, no quotes or statements from either Wolves or the Alex. It was the usual story of one bookmaker slashing odds and the rest getting twitchy.

Still, it was a messy situation at Molineux. Wolves had dismissed four managers in just fifteen months. They had just been relegated from the Championship and would be lining up against the Alex. It was a club in turmoil. And yet Davis was a boyhood fan, and when a club is in your blood it's hard to discount. Even saddled with debts, Wolves could attract players from all over the world. League One was a blip, and they needed a manager to take them straight back up. But as the news broke, I wondered if Davis was ready. He'd had two very successful seasons, but getting out of the next division was a different matter.

In the race to fill the position Davis was in illustrious company. The experienced Kenny Jackett and ex-England manager Steve McClaren were also being "considered" if you believed the bookmakers' odds. The newspaper columns even mentioned Wolves chairman Steve Morgan being a fan of the Crewe manager and everything that he had achieved. That added credibility to the stories that soon spread.

JUDAS!

This is when I first heard the comment. A pretty standard modern-day definition would be "an individual whom sells out his/her friends for their own personal benefit".

Was that a fair description of the Crewe manager, because a club had expressed an interest in his services? He was installed as the favourite for the job; therefore he had no loyalty to Crewe. That was the gist of the conversation, at least from some of the group in the pub. It was over the top, uncalled for and misinformed. It was, however, fascinating how quickly some supporters turned on him.

In fact, although he did meet the Molineux Chief Executive Jez Moxey, Davis did not instigate the contact. He was flattered by the interest, and both he and Neil Baker saw it as a fantastic opportunity (they would have gone as a management duo, I believe). But like the Burnley situation, it would have been a testing transition with huge responsibility. Wolves had to get it right. Davis was the new kid on the block, an exciting prospect that might, just might, continue his run of great form. But they needed something more concrete. If Davis had taken Crewe out of League One then I reckon he would have been nailed on for either the Burnley or Wolves job. As things stood, he still had much to prove at Gresty Road, especially when compared to his predecessor Gradi.

Before the Molineux situation was resolved, there was an interesting line from Gradi that also raised eyebrows and left us wondering if Davis really was about to leave. 'I am happy not to be doing the job and if, for instance, Steve were to go and they said to me will you be caretaker I'd say yeah for about three weeks,' he told *The Crewe Chronicle*. It was a strange comment, but evidence that the Alex had considered the implications. It wasn't a point-blank "no" from Gradi, as he would never let the club down. But he wasn't needed. Wolves chose Kenny Jackett. Davis missed out, and he was disappointed. We breathed another sigh of relief!

***

The Wolves snub meant that Davis had to dust himself down and concentrate on matters at Gresty Road. That almost suggests that he had to settle for second best, and that he somehow came crawling back with his tail between his legs. That's way off the mark. There were no bad feelings. It was business as usual. John Bowler and Gradi were thankful that they had not been forced to instigate another management hunt.

There were a few Alex fans left smarting, still unhappy that Davis had even contemplated the move. They still saw it as disloyalty. This left me pondering the whole situation and whether Davis, the club or the supporters had got things out of perspective.

The over-riding question that needs addressing is whether wanting to manage at the highest level makes any manager disloyal? Of course it doesn't. There are many reasons for wanting to move on.

Without revealing figures, Davis is one of the lowest-paid managers in League One. Few would dispute that. And who in their right mind would continue with an employer who consistently devalued their services? That's not the case at Gresty Road, as the limited budget is such that players or the manager cannot be easily awarded pay rises while attendances remain static around the 4,000 mark. However, Davis brought serious cash into the club by winning promotion, and secured a further financial boost by winning the Johnstone's Paint Trophy. Those unbeaten runs played a significant part in attracting the attention of scouts. They saw competent, skilful and winning players in action. The values rocketed. Surely he's due a pay rise!

I jest of course, because Davis doesn't do it solely for money. He's a real football man. He started his professional playing career at Crewe, and likewise with his stint in full-time management. Unlike most managers who might come to the club, he is in tune with the overall ethos. He wouldn't stitch us up, and he wouldn't just walk out. He talks regularly with the chairman. They have enjoyed a solid relationship from the beginning. Both are realistic men.

But has the club short-changed Davis? In the background, there have been financial adjustments that have, in my opinion, impacted significantly on the manager's budget. Over several years a number of loans have been made from Crewe Alexandra to companies owned by (or linked to) one of the Alex directors. The sums involved are substantial. As of summer 2014, I was informed that the loans had been cleared. Although interest was paid to the club, it was often a substantial sum that could have seen two or three players brought in. John Bowler told me that the transfer and wage budget was never restricted because of the loans, although priority was always given to funding the academy. He would always put the club's youth set-up ahead of other spending. So we have been forced to cut our cloth accordingly. I can't help feeling that the monies involved could and should have been used specifically for first team purposes. But that's my opinion.

For Davis, investment in the playing staff will always be a luxury. He needed it after the play-off victory in 2012, when we had momentum on our side. I think that he would have loved to kick-on, and attempted back-to-back promotions. That would only have been possible if the club had the financial muscle to retain players like Nick Powell and Ashley Westwood on lucrative contracts. Even then, that would not guarantee keeping them at Crewe. It always has been a delicate balancing act. Alex fans know all-too well that the chairman has always been mindful of over-committing the club, saddling ourselves with a wage debt that can prove a real burden when a club drops down a division. So it's easy to appreciate his concerns.

But where does that leave a manager hungry for further success? Supporters would also love to enjoy a jolly back into the Championship, like old times under Gradi. Instead we're left in limbo and in a situation of stalemate. Davis must accept that under the current framework he will never be given millions to spend. He has a modest budget and an academy from which to pluck talent. Although it's a better situation than many managers find themselves in, how long could someone work away knowing that his ambitions must remain tethered?

The only outcome is Davis eventually being tempted by a club that can and will offer him the chance to reach for the stars. Like every player, he will have the Premier League in his long-term sights. Managing at the highest level is that ultimate goal. Much as it pains me to say it, unless a fairy godmother millionaire drops in, Crewe Alexandra is unlikely to fulfil such aspirations.

In everyday life we all encounter problems. We deal with them, re-adjust and put mechanisms in place to avoid similar issues in the future. If the demands become too great, and when expectation is heaped too high, many struggle to function. In football circles there is always pressure, from one week to the next. When a manager has done everything in his power to address and overcome those challenges, he is likely to seek support from those around him - namely the chairman. Kind words and "backing" are fine, but progression up the leagues these days involves cash. At Crewe that has always been in short supply. There has been enough to survive and keep pace, but never enough to challenge the frontrunners each season.

Davis performed miracles across his first eighteen months and on a limited budget. Why wouldn't that attract a number of clubs interested in his services? He didn't quite manage to craft a silk purse from a pig's ear and keep rising up the divisions, but he did an admirable job. He knew from day one that he wouldn't be given limitless funds to chase promotion to the Championship, so he quite reasonably explored the options available. He didn't walk out, he always kept the chairman informed and, ultimately, he continued working, planning and trying to progress the squad at his disposal.

In many ways he will have wished that he had jumped ship and taken anything on offer; his third season was about to become testing beyond belief.

CORNWALL

A sign of the times is that I first heard about the Cornwall fiasco via Twitter. It was about 11:30am on Sunday 7th July 2013, the Alex had wrapped up a decent pre-season training camp and everyone was looking forward to the warm-up games back at Gresty Road over the following weeks. Then the Internet exploded. There'd been a serious incident. I caught a comment from someone who knew one of the backroom staff, hazy details but still very concerning.

Websites carried details about five Crewe Alexandra players who had been arrested. The headlines were shockers, some shouting "sexual assault" while others hit harder with "rape" as the allegation. In the following days, the printed press caught up. The case gifted them a dramatic line of enquiry. The story would dominate the news.

It was unbelievable, one of those double-take moments. This kind of thing didn't happen at Crewe. I looked at the reports in utter disbelief. Was this genuine, had our players really dragged the club's name through the mud?

For a few days I shut down. Not only did I not want to believe it, there was a strong desire to avoid getting dragged into the sorry mess. It was a bloody nightmare, but also a reporter's dream. The column inches grew quickly, although nobody seemed to have all of the facts. An email arrived asking for my thoughts, an invitation to pen a column on the subject, or to call back and give a few quotes. Absolutely no chance, I thought. It was bad enough already. Without details or confirmation about the players involved, my input could only make things worse. So I held back, even keeping clear of the online threads that Alex fans were already populating.

So what actually happened? Well, without outlining parts of the case that I remain unclear about myself, here's what I know and have been told. On the Friday evening, with players and staff winding down at the team hotel near Redruth, most were chilling out and enjoying a few drinks. The mini-tour of Cornwall had been a huge success. Everyone was knackered. Some of the players were already heading to bed. Then one of the remaining lads approached Steve Davis and Neil Baker, asking if it was okay to take a group out for a few late drinks.

Why wouldn't it have been alright? They had worked hard and deserved it. They were given a few quid from the drinks kitty and told to get back before the usual curfew. That was the last anyone saw of them that night.

Who knows exactly where they all went, who they met along the way and where they finished up? The end result was a knock on the gaffer's hotel room door very early on the Saturday morning. The officer needed a word. Mr. Davis needed to look at some images and pick out the men he recognised. He was told that his players were in custody, arrested for an alleged assault on a young woman. A case was now ongoing, and it developed fast.

Oh to be a fly on the window of the team coach as it drove back north that day! A few hours later, two further players were arrested when they arrived back in Cheshire. They were also wanted for questioning about the events of the previous night. The initial police statement detailed only the ages and addresses (just the town) of those being questioned, but even Inspector Clouseau could have worked out which players were in the frame. It made the BBC website and was carried by several national newspapers. The club was major news by Monday morning.

More locally, it was the lead item on *The Warrington Guardian's* website, complete with a photograph of one of those allegedly involved. The player concerned just happened to come from that town, and that was sufficient reason for the editor to splash the player's face (but not his name) and a few basic details about the accusations beneath. Harsh, to say the least, especially with the word "RAPE" grabbing readers' attention before they had chance to digest what might have actually happened down in Cornwall. The reality was that nobody had all of the facts.

When I had come to terms with the grisly situation, my mind switched to Davis. I wonder how hard his jaw hit the floor when he listened to the allegations. It wasn't his fault, surely, but he'd been in charge of the players during that tour of Cornwall. It was only natural for him to feel responsible. After all, he was a father of two young men also involved in football. One of them had been part of Crewe's pre-season preparations down on the south west coast. And that was my next thought. Did the manager at any point worry that his lad, Harry, had been part of the group arrested? In those horrendous moments with the police officer, before he had identified any of the players or had chance to check hotel rooms, was there any doubt in his mind? I asked this a few weeks after the event, when we explored the father-son(s) relationship as part of the ongoing biography project. Even then, with dust settled and many aspects of the case much clearer, Davis was still in shock. His lad, however, had not concerned him. He was one of the players that had chosen to get an early night; they had spoken in the hotel lounge bar.

By now we had seven players in the spotlight, released without charge, but with an investigation pending. They returned to Reaseheath for training, but what a strained atmosphere that must have been. Perhaps there were accusing looks from team mates, offers of support from some, or cold shoulders from others? To compound matters, anyone in the hotel that night saw their mobile phones and cameras confiscated. They were needed by the Devon and Cornwall Police who were sifting through evidence, trying to piece together what had happened that night. This affected many innocent people, as some of the lads had precious family memories recorded on their devices. There were photos of new-born babies, happy times at parties and general life snaps that made them smile each day. Now they were gone; because of the actions of a minority. I bet they were livid.

Away from the club, the kangaroo court was in full swing. Although it remains a vocal minority, it is hard to ignore the comments, messages and status updates that flood the Internet forums. That happens each week, usually involving gripes about team selections or the Alex missing out on another player because of wage constraints. But this was dynamite, and discussions and arguments reached fever pitch. Once it was the pub, face-to-face conversations over a pint, maybe neighbours swapping gossip over the fence. Back then it was relatively contained, even when tittle-tattle swept through a factory shop floor. It was usually done and dusted in days. The local newspaper would carry the story later that week, but would be tossed away with the rubbish soon after. It was yesterday's news before you knew it. In 2013 that was never going to happen.

I felt for John Bowler, the chairman, and countless other club officials who must have dreaded going into work on the Monday morning. They were the frontline and would be forced to handle the fallout. Put yourself in their shoes and imagine going into the office, factory or even college, knowing that someone beside you or in the same room had been arrested on suspicion of such a terrible act. They were allegations, and no charges had been made. But still, people make instant judgements and take sides. Right or wrong, that is human nature. Such opinions were evident where I work. A couple of colleagues were very clear: they would not tolerate working with someone who had been arrested for an alleged sexual assault. They would insist that they were removed; else they would walk out. The majority didn't know, as it's one of those situations that you must experience before you can fully understand the kaleidoscope of emotions involved. Only a couple of people sided with the law (Presumption of

Innocence), which states that the players implicated were innocent until proven guilty. For some that was hard to swallow.

Back to the Internet chatter and many Alex fans were outraged. The immediate reaction was twofold: the players were guilty and should be sacked, at least suspended and dropped from the squad; or those involved were innocent until proven guilty and, until any court case was concluded, life should go on. Of those prepared to state an opinion, few sat on the fence. It was black or white. Those shouting loudest believed that the "guilty" (in their opinion) players had tarnished the good name of Crewe Alexandra. It wasn't acceptable. Davis needed to act, and quickly.

Unfortunately, there have been several very unsavoury incidents involving footballers in recent years. They are yobs, over-paid hooligans, out of control and above the law according to some. High-profile cases caught on camera put some of the top-paid "stars" on a murky pedestal alongside investment bankers and their hefty bonus payments. Now a few Alex players joined them. "There's no smoke without fire" must have been spouted a thousand times by supporters keen to have their say.

For Davis, this wasn't a simple fire fight. In the days and weeks after the incident, he dealt with players, their families, agents, the media, and of course he had to keep the chairman and other key club officials in the loop as things happened. I know that he spent much of July on the phone, placating, reassuring and comforting, as well as speaking to the police as and when required. And if "words" were exchanged between players, he had to jump on them before things escalated. I'm sure there was bitterness in the aftermath, as mud sticks and those not involved were probably desperate to distance themselves from the ones under the spotlight.

There was never likely to be a quick-fix, an easy way to resolve this messy situation. Many sexual assault cases - some allegations of crimes going back years - have been headline news in recent years. They have to be handled carefully. Both prosecution and defence must uncover every last detail. The Alex players were not going to see their case brushed under any carpet. It was to be a long, drawn-out investigation.

I'm sure groups of footballers have found themselves in compromising situations since the game began more than a century ago. They are celebrities, always have been, often part of an innocent photo opportunity. In some cases they are trophies for others determined to join the glitzy football scene.

However, before we go any further, it is important to acknowledge that a 22-year-old woman was involved in Cornwall. She must have felt wronged and wanted to take the matter to the police. We were not there that night. We must respect her right to seek justice.

Sadly, when news broke about the incident, plenty of Alex fans shrugged. It was not a surprise to some. In the months leading up to the Saturday night excesses, there had been a worrying trend developing. Some of the players were eagerly uploading photos, comments and, in a few cases, what supporters thought were inappropriate messages - on Twitter in particular. There were crude gags, daft pictures of trashed hotel rooms and even high jinks alongside the team bus that broke down en route to the training camp. It was a bad omen.

Most of these online accounts, especially those of high-profile sports and entertainment stars, carry a disclaimer. They state that the content and opinion is that of the user and not the views of their paymaster or umbrella organisation. I'm not sure that some of the squad grasped this, posing in team colours and happily stating that they played football for Crewe Alexandra. I wondered if anyone from the club was monitoring what was being said (they do now, what both players and supporters are saying). Fans love being able to engage with their heroes, but the boundaries seem to be lower than ever. In some cases, there were none.

And that leads us to the next, very interesting question: would Dario Gradi have done anything differently? In fact, would the Cornwall incident have occurred with him in charge of the first team?

Unfortunately, it is almost impossible comparing things over time. Everything changes, especially technology. These days there is no place to hide. I have many memories stretching across nearly four decades that involve players, but hardly any were taped, pictured or videoed. When I was a teenager they were the coolest men alive, playing football for a living and attracting attention wherever they went. But they only posed for photos if there was one of the journalists around on matchday.

Then in my twenties it somehow gave you credibility to be associated with the players. Leaving a pub to head to a night spot you knew you'd get in because the doormen recognised them, or inside the venue you too would get a free pint. It is all shallow stuff, and rather embarrassing looking back on those hanger-on days.

Later still, with writing and football-related research in full flow, it was very handy knowing a man who knew. So I became acquainted with a few of them. There was never a time when I wanted to become friends, but it was always fascinating listening to those on the inside of the game and watching them outside of their comfort zone.

There were punch-ups, extra-marital affairs and buying/selling things down the pub. They did it all in the 1980s and 90s, and it is amazing that some of the antics I witnessed or heard second-hand did not lead to allegations or even charges. But it was a different time, few had access to the information that we all take for granted these days. Even pre-season tours were, largely speaking, kept private. Many reading these pages will recall the good old days under Gradi when a July jolly to Dublin was the norm. Two or three games, often St. Patrick's and a university side, then relaxation, fans and players mingling, enjoying a few pints, out later in the pubs, restaurants and clubs. Everyone went home at night, safely tucked up and ready for a light jog in the morning. Or did they?

And then back in Nantwich, when I returned from London in 1997, there was another generation of players looking to enjoy the trappings of well-paid sportsmen. My first few seasons during that fabulous Championship era were spent drinking alongside Alex "stars" of the time, young men who should not have been out supping lager until 2:00am before training or, in a couple of cases, on the eve of important games. They were just out for a laugh, happy to chat with fans in the pubs. They recognised faces from the crowd, from club events, and I suppose like anyone else in life they welcomed the company. For some high-profile players I suspect it can be a very lonely existence, especially the younger ones.

The Crewe players of my "youth" avoided trouble largely speaking, but within a couple of seasons those "bad eggs" were all sold or released. The explanation was, in most cases, that Gradi had found out about the excesses and would not tolerate players that fell short of his very high standards. He was always a tough taskmaster. Even when they performed on matchday, scored goals and won games, well, that never seemed to be enough for the man. He was no tyrant, but he took no prisoners. Those situations were soon resolved. Gradi got shot of them. Their names were not plastered across the Internet or even on the back page of *The Crewe Chronicle*. Things were "dealt" with. They became former Crewe Alexandra players - no more, no less. Few people ever found out that there had been a problem. Just the fans suffered, as usual, left wondering why favourite players had become surplus to requirements when they were seemingly at their peak.

Not so long ago there was only news on the main terrestrial TV channels. Satellite channels were limited and nobody had mobile phones. Footballers were not on the small screen 24/7 and celebrated the world over, as they are now. Top-flight players earned good money, but their salaries were modest compared to today's multi-millionaires. Lower division footballers dipped under the radar, relatively free to come and go as they pleased. The new devices that now offer untold connectivity have only become widely available and affordable in the last decade; that has put them all under the microscope.

Like it or not, that explosion of information and access to data and images coincides with the first time that Gradi looked to step aside, circa 2006/07. That is when the first iPhone arrived, and a multitude of other smart phones soon after. So the goalposts were moving, and perhaps it was one of the reasons that encouraged the Alex legend to kick-start the succession planning. Gradi has never shied away from technology, but the proliferation of mobiles, tablets and laptops offering access to a dazzling array of media must have set him thinking. A decade earlier his players would have been focused 100% across the working day. They arrived, trained and then went home. What they did away from the club was their own business, within reason. Besides, if they did step over the mark they were rarely caught.

Fast-forward a few years and the Alex first team lads were fully wired. They checked news feed in their cars, swapped texts and uploaded statuses in the dressing room, laughed and posted pictures to Facebook over lunch. Like any office or strict home, there were rules about usage. But the phones were always there, lurking somewhere in the background. Gradi did not have them on short leashes any more.

So no, I don't think that Gradi could have prevented Cornwall. Davis and Bakes are no pushovers, but they are operating against a new set of rules, with a wholly different generation of young men. They have more cash in their pockets, and increasingly the players on loan from the top-flight bring with them big-city attitude, habits and influences.

***

Football goes on. Within days of the club attracting so much unwanted attention in the summer of 2013, it was time to step outside of the protective Reaseheath bubble. There were friendly games to honour, and Davis made an interesting comment. He declared that anyone "fit to play" would travel to the match away at Norton in Staffordshire. Everyone wondered whether that meant physically or mentally fit, as anyone at the centre of the furore would have struggled to keep a level head. It would have affected training, time with families and most certainly any involvement out on the pitch.

There was not, thankfully, a media scrum at Norton's compact ground in Smallthorne. Had the allegations been levelled at Manchester United, Chelsea or Liverpool, there would have been hundreds of written and photojournalists clambering for a scoop. But this was a Crewe friendly, being played at a sleepy non-league venue. The local media turned up, looking for snippets to fill the sports pages. But they never intended to give Davis or his players a rough ride. Everyone knew that the situation was delicate. It was best left alone.

There were still online comments; mainly nasty prods here, aggressive pokes there. Some felt strong enough to vilify the manager for including the players under suspicion in his pre-season plans. But what else could he do? It is a squad game, more so now than ever before. Davis had to find his best team, and there was the Luke Murphy role to fill - or at least work around. The players would need to be ready for August regardless. He stood by them.

As I contemplated this chapter, I sought advice from my good friend Mark Potts. An author of several local books, he had also followed the Alex across many years. Between us we decided that it was pointless naming the players implicated. The names had been splattered across the Internet and, in some cases, within the pages of the printed press. It was standard procedure to carry basic details in police statements (ages and addresses, etc) but no more. When the case was resolved one way or another the names would be there for all to see. If they were found not guilty then they should be allowed to get on with their lives. Recording who, what and where as part of the *After Dario* story would achieve little, only make permanent the allegations for future supporters to see. So I moved on and considered what the Cornwall effect had on the new season.

COME ON YOU REDS!

And so to the Rotherham curtain raiser, played out in the customary blaze of early August sunshine... as things stood, it could have been a nightmare for the lads being investigated. And let's not forget the fans, especially the more highly-strung "yoofs" in the Gresty Road end that stood and yelled alongside the nearest away fans. It would have been very easy for the visiting Yorkshire hordes to taunt, poke fun and insult the Alex because of what happened in July. Football fans have a habit of finding the weak spot, prodding away and tipping either players or rival supporters over the emotional edge. They didn't, thankfully, and there was no collective chanting. There were random comments, but I heard as many from Crewe fans who were themselves unhappy to see certain men part of the matchday squad. But it wasn't their decision. Davis picked the team. He wanted a winning start.

To be fair, it was a cracking game to launch the 2013/14 campaign. But for the Alex there was so much riding on the result that day. There were demons to bury. Players had points to prove. Supporters needed to get over preconceptions and opinions formed in previous weeks, when everything connected to the sexual assault allegations remained hazy. The police investigation was ongoing. We needed to know whether our form would be affected.

On the pitch, the Alex squad managed to block out details of the case, forget lengthy sessions answering questions and maybe shrug off withering looks from team mates; at least during the first half. The opening phase was frantic, exciting and could not have gone any better. After three minutes we had the lead. Anthony Grant was the unlikely hero, the summer signing from Stevenage lashed a super shot from outside the box and watched a cheeky deflection send the ball sailing past the Millers' goalkeeper. Seven minutes later Max Clayton slipped past his marker, latched onto AJ Leitch-Smith's pass and grabbed Crewe's second. The Rotherham contingent was shell-shocked; but not for long. A minute later it was 2-1; a wild long-range shot gave Alan Martin no chance in the Alex goal. It was an insane start. The fans were up for it, and the stadium rocked. For a while, all negativity was brushed aside, especially when Ryan Colclough was tripped and Harry Davis converted a 48th minute penalty. It was job done, three points, and no need to worry about anything...

HOME AND DRY?

If only football was that easy. Rotherham gaffer Steve "*in yer face*" Evans reacted immediately, as any manager worth his salt should. They were playing away, trailing by two goals, so there was nothing to lose. They had to at least give the travelling Millers something to cheer about; that is a general rule of thumb. He made two immediate substitutions and the game changed. In a flash the Alex were on the back foot. There was wave after wave of pressure; chances, goalmouth scrambles, shots wide, and near misses. The Alex rallied and really should have wrapped things up. It was cracking entertainment, the value for money we all crave - and a win to boot, we thought!

So as time ticked by we sat back to enjoy the spectacle. It was a proper ding-dong encounter, with Evans increasingly animated on the touchline. He took the jeers and jibes in his stride, wiping sweat off his brow after each outburst at the fourth official, or Davis and his staff.

The Alex should have parked the bus, as most now describe locking things down and defending a lead these days. But defenders Mark Ellis and Thierry Audel remained on the bench. That was a mistake. On 86 minutes we conceded, an impressive curling shot that once again gave Alan Martin no chance. Still, we were 3-2 up; just four minutes to go. Keep the ball, that's all we had to do. It was frenetic, worrying and unbearable. Davis signalled to the substitutes warming up down by the corner flag. Then he started hollering. He needed them - quickly! Vadaine Oliver and Ollie Turton got ready, flung tracksuits aside and waited for a break in play. The referee waved them on. There was a minute on the clock. Off came Max Clayton and Byron Moore.

TICK, TOCK, TICK, TOCK...

It was almost over. Then the board went up. More time added on. It was mayhem, a final surge from Rotherham, panic defending by Crewe, Davis and Bakes going berserk at the referee, pointing at their watches.

Somehow, with intuition that only football supporters possess, we just knew it was coming. Another long throw, this time deep into the Alex box. In it went, bobbled and evaded despairing Alex lunges. They equalised deep into stoppage time! Evans bounced his ample frame down the touchline and ran onto the pitch, hugging his players. Some of the visiting fans could not contain themselves and danced onto the turf and straight into the arms of awaiting police officers and Alex stewards. Gutted does not properly describe how the majority of the 5,296 felt as they streamed out of the ground.

Then came the recriminations; we needed to make sense of it all. The attackers and midfielders should have been the first line of defence. They were found wanting. They still gave 100%, but that wasn't enough to stem the tide of conceded goals and, ultimately, points thrown away. New-boy Grant was immense, covering every blade of grass. But that was also quickly forgotten. The ding-dong draw felt as though we'd lost. The demons of defeat were everywhere. The players obviously couldn't deal with the allegations in the background. They had let the fans down. It wasn't a good start.

That (four-minute) collapse resonated with supporters. Three goals should have been enough, but we crumbled. Even at that very early stage, with the season just beginning, there was concern. Was Murphy's departure likely to prove catastrophic, and would the Cornwall case play too heavy on the players' minds to allow day-to-day operations to run smoothly?

Some of the answers came over the next seven days. Bury tipped the Alex out of the League Cup. Then at Milton Keynes Dons, a 0-1 reverse only served to mask various issues. It wasn't a heavy defeat; it was on the road, so alarm bells did not start ringing. But there seemed to be friction between some players, arguments about positions, who should provide cover, and accusations that others did not distribute the ball effectively. On the pitch, the finger pointing had started. For the modest travelling support it was a disappointment, but not the end of the world. There was always next week.

The jury (i.e. the supporters back at Gresty Road) convened the following Saturday and presided over the game vs Tranmere. It was a chance to put points on the board. In front of another decent crowd, it was the perfect opportunity for the players to show unity and resolve. They did, and the 2-1 victory gave everyone breathing space, but it was no showcase performance.

With less than ten minutes to play it was still tense, the Alex clinging on to the lead. Rovers were down to ten men from mid-way through the first half, and yet we couldn't punish them further and make the numerical advantage count. Much like the point against Rotherham, the three earned that day pulled a veil over problems that were looming large on the horizon.

What followed was a wretched period, a seven-match winless streak that stretched to mid-October. Leyton Orient beat us comfortably 2-0, Swindon put five past us, and then a couple of draws interrupted embarrassing 3-0 home defeats to Walsall and Gillingham. Okay, I exaggerate, as a 1-0 JPT win over Accrington broke that sequence. But as the 1980s TV milk advert "Accrington Stanley… who are they?" once asked somewhat sarcastically, this was no cause for celebration. The fact that we remained in that competition and had the chance to defend the trophy (never done, by the way) was a very small crumb of comfort, as the bread-and-butter league games had gone stale. No matter how we tried to dress it, the season was going down the toilet.

Interestingly, before the meltdown, at the League Managers' Awards night in May 2013, Alex chairman John Bowler stood up and praised his young manager for his incredible achievements since taking charge. He also said that he would be there for Davis, through thick and thin, during the bad times as well as good. And there would, he emphasised, be bad times. It was as though he had a crystal ball. Months later that support must have been heartening. Davis knew that he had the chairman's full backing, a rare commodity in English football. And it was genuine. Many come out and splash their support in the media, before twisting the knife in the background. Bowler rarely issues statements to the press, which has been a source of frustration to supporters over the years. The mouthpiece was always Gradi. The Alex chairman doesn't interfere. And yet he is always there: listening, thinking practically and logically, setting up the next five and ten-year plans.

With nothing going right for Crewe, Davis needed strong men around him. Neil Baker was one, and the calm influence of Bowler must have been a tremendously comforting force. The support structure was there, but much of the leg work was done by the manager. Each week he kept faith in struggling players, giving those men chances and searching tirelessly to find the elusive winning formula. I am sure that many will disagree, but in my opinion Davis handled the situation as well as could be expected. This wasn't his fault. The gaffer could have hit out, forced sales or at least got players out on loan. But that's not his style. He confronted them and worked to achieve what was best for the team, talking, cajoling, trying to build confidence and managing the reaction of others as best he could. In many ways his hands were tied.

Had the "accused" brought the club's name into disrepute? Maybe, but they had not been charged. And in terms of cover, there was never a big budget to quickly strengthen the squad. Davis had to juggle, he had to fix things, and he had to go with those emotionally damaged players. The bottom line is that certain players could and should have acted more responsibly. There was bad luck, injuries and then the unyielding spiral of defeat pulling already dispirited players down. We, the fans, suffered as the results went against the Alex week after week.

On a wholly different level, the situation reminded me of Eric Cantona back in 1995. The infamous Manchester United player's Kung-Fu kick on a Crystal Palace supporter caused international outrage. That, too, was a police matter. Sir Alex Ferguson revealed many years later that his first reaction had been to sack the Frenchman. He brought shame on the club and his actions were cause for dismissal. The case differed from Crewe's in that Cantona's outburst was captured on live TV. But Ferguson bit his tongue, took advice from others, and acted as a father figure would when his son was being hunted down. Thankfully, the Alex avoided such widespread media coverage, but the protective blanket was still required. Davis wrapped up his players and guided them through one of the most traumatic periods of the club's history.

So, did Cornwall have an adverse effect on the team (and club) as a whole in those months immediately after the summer? I'd say yes, it most certainly did, and deep into the season the players and management were still trying to recover the situation. I doubt anyone could push such serious accusations to the back of their head. Reputations were at stake. I suspect there were many heated conversations, with colleagues pointing the finger at each other. There must have been some serious fall-outs, players and staff possibly threatening to walk out? If similar had occurred at another club then maybe there would have been a more dramatic outcome. But this was Crewe. There was a culture of stability, sensible people making considered decisions. It had to be dealt with. Nobody could make it all go away but, slowly but surely, we got through it. We had to.

BACKLASH

How the worm sometimes turns! William Shakespeare coined that phrase, effectively stating that even the meekest and most unassuming creature will, if pushed into an awkward corner, eventually lash out and fight back. Alex fans have been a placid bunch for many years, accepting that under Dario Gradi at least we had to appreciate that every now and then we'd get knocked down. There was always a cautious optimism that we'd bounce back, that exciting new players would emerge and that we'd soon enjoy good times. So we cut him plenty of slack. That changed when duties were handed to Steve Holland, and again before the succession to Steve Davis. But I never expected supporters to turn on the new man so soon, especially after two visits to Wembley.

They did. I think the manager's brief links to Burnley and Wolves didn't help, as covered in an earlier chapter. But as the Cornwall situation dragged on, with no resolution either way, tempers began to flare. Results remained inconsistent right through September, with just a couple of draws offering supporters any hope. It was not much to cling on to. There was barely a hint of revival. When there were green shoots, they were quickly trodden down. The Murphy-free midfield continued to flounder and the under-pressure defence creaked and cracked further.

The winless stretch had alarmed, confused and alienated fans to such an extent that I thought we were close to a repeat of the "Holland Out" campaign. Saying that, almost a year on, it seems utterly crazy. There was no comparison, and yet the natives were very restless. It was always a handful of big-mouths, supporters prepared to shout above the crowd. But they were heard. Those critical and often abusive voices were easily picked out. And in many ways they had a point. Football is about results. There is only so long a watching public can tolerate failure, no matter what came before.

The rest were largely silent, suffering as goals rained in and passes went astray. At home to Gillingham at the tail-end of September, the management looked on bemused. They had tried everything, but each failure was highlighted and thrown back in their faces. Matchday attendances held up surprisingly well, but when the Gills' third goal beat Steve Phillips there was a mass exodus.

FIRE DRILL!

The main stand was almost deserted when the final whistle put the players out of their misery. That's how the majority showed their displeasure. The few who remained dished out more vitriol than usual. The Alex players rushed to the relative safety of the dressing room, although Davis and Baker were hot on their heels. Words needed to be said.

October proved to be the most testing of months, and trying to assess the damage and run a few repairs proved increasingly problematic. The squad on offer to Davis had been relatively settled. Few had been out long-term injured apart from Mathias Pogba. However, of the new arrivals, the likes of Lee Molyneux, Thierry Audel, Anthony Grant and Jon Guthrie had shown glimpses of potential, but did not provide the impact either the manager or the fans craved. None of the fringe players were knocking down the gaffer's door demanding or deserving to play. Even potential match winners Max Clayton, Vadaine Oliver and Ryan Colclough disappointed, collectively contributing just four goals across the first ten league games of the season.

In midfield there had been little contribution on the goal front. Grant scored on the opening day, that dramatic but hugely disappointing draw that set the tone. We couldn't hang on to leads, and in games where the Alex fell a goal behind we didn't recover even a point. It was psychological, it had to be. The players knew each other and many had stepped out together on that historical last day at home to Walsall just a few months earlier. Now it looked as though they had all met up an hour before kick-off!

The reaction from the sidelines was consistent, though. The ongoing woes were down to abject failure at the back; that was the general consensus in the pubs pre-match. Shouts from the crowd questioned the team selection, suggesting that the wrong players were being given opportunities. It nearly always involved the defence. The manager played his son Harry (21 years old) alongside George Ray (19) in the first four league encounters. It was a central partnership that boasted height but not power, and certainly lacked an understanding. That takes time and games. Numerous supporters raised concerns, adamant that such a young pairing would be bullied by the experienced journeymen strikers of League One. But when Mark Ellis was recalled (at the expense of Ray) there was no immediate transformation.

FIVE-NIL!

Swindon went nap and smashed five past Crewe; supporters were left dazed. They didn't blame Ellis; he battled, tackled and stuck his head in where it hurts. Such qualities often win over supporters, and quite rightly so. Instead they looked for a common denominator. Why did we concede so many goals? Although the left and right-sided defenders were rotated across the next five matches (Ollie Turton, on-loan Gregor Robertson, Kelvin Mellor, Matt Tootle and Jon Guthrie) nothing clicked. The Alex lost three and drew twice with Davis and Ellis working together. The frustrations continued to simmer and many wondered if the gaffer actually knew his best line-up.

So by now the Davis-Ellis partnership was the focus of fan fury, with most demanding to see Adam Dugdale returned to the team. But the dissatisfaction went deeper than that. Some said it out loud; others just wished that Davis would remove his son from the starting line-up. It was a case of heart ruling head. The supporters just needed a target and the manager's son was the victim. Dugdale, meanwhile, had been a great servant, but his mind was still elsewhere for very personal reasons. He'd been out on loan at Tranmere since August. But at Prenton Park, the Alex defender did not gain much confidence, just a little match practice. In the five games he played, Rovers lost four and drew one. And yet many Crewe fans persisted with their calls for his return at the expense of Davis.

Throwing accusations of nepotism was cheap and easy. The manager largely avoided the issue when questioned. He picked his strongest team, he always told us. He and Baker watched them in training and made the decisions that would, they hoped, turn things around. The fans only saw the end product on matchday. In my opinion, Davis never did favour his son; he maintained that his chosen combination took heed of instructions. They were the best pairing. The others did not listen. When they did, any pre-match advice was forgotten soon after kick-off. That cut no ice with the prime movers demanding changes. While results went against Crewe, the unhappy fans insisted that reshuffling the defence was imperative. Those calls grew louder each week.

The collective wish was granted away at Notts County. It wasn't enough for some, as the tweak was enforced; Davis (junior) was ruled out with a knock sustained against Gillingham. So Dugdale was recalled from Prenton Park to partner Ellis at the heart of the Crewe defence, although when the gutsy combo stepped out at Meadow Lane there were sneers in the background as the team took their positions. Being "forced" into a change was not what they had wanted. The manager was running scared, they suggested. Some fans had made their minds up; Davis was not the long-term answer for Crewe Alexandra. They felt that he was not making the right decisions. He'd had it too easy when the team was winning. It made for depressing debate between games, and some of the conversations were pointless. They had no foundation. The results had been poor; no, they had been shocking. But as we have seen, many factors had caused a maelstrom. Davis and the players had been sucked in. Fans barracking from the sidelines were not going to help. We all needed to be strong, but it was an increasingly painful experience.

The Cornwall incident was bad enough, but rumours of troublesome players and unrest within the camp sent fans' tongues into overdrive. In the Nottingham pubs prior to the County fixture I heard a couple of lads suggest that Davis had "lost" the dressing room. The stories were vague, but it was rumoured that two or three players had overstepped the mark on the Reaseheath training pitches. They were unsettling others; they had become cocky and questioned the manager's authority, even challenged him about decisions. That was a bad influence on the younger kids breaking through from the academy. Nobody knew if this was true, but those whispers soon grew in volume.

TALK, TALK!

Players talk; fans talk. Davis revealed nothing ahead of the game at Meadow Lane, but his position was made decidedly tricky when the home side banged four past a Crewe side that had no answers. The occasional attacks led by Clayton, Oliver and Moore once again came to nothing. Even the fresh legs of Colclough, Aneke and Inman failed to produce even a consolation strike that would have given the supporters something to cling on to. Davis was using every weapon at his disposal, but to no avail. Two goals in each half for the hosts did the damage, and the Alex manager was now an easy target for the boo boys. It was inconceivable to think that he was now working against the clock, but similar form under Holland and Thordarson had started the countdown to dismissal - and at about the same time of the year.

As the goals against tally rose at an alarming rate, there were knee-jerk calls for Davis to sort out his defence. I say "knee-jerk" because there was no real logic behind the complaints. The back four was unsettled, and there were reasons for that; they were the obvious department to blame. It was the manager's job to sort the problems out, knock heads together and stop an unexpected and very unwelcome rot. He was, after all, a defender by trade. Why couldn't he get it right? But this was a team issue. The midfield and attack were culpable, not offering enough support to the beleaguered stoppers. I think that the gaffer could have shuffled his right, left and central defenders every match and still not found the perfect formula.

The Johnstone's Paint Trophy was the tiniest ray of sunshine in a dull and wet month. It was the opportunity to start another charge to Wembley. A cup run, the chance to make history and retain the trophy, and hopefully drag the league form kicking and screaming with us. Accrington Stanley in the first round had been the last Alex victory, and that was surely an omen. So with true football-fan logic applied, when Crewe travelled to Stanley's Lancashire neighbours Fleetwood Town there was plenty of optimism - despite the appalling recent form. It was completely unfounded, a set of supporters desperate for something - ANYTHING - to breathe life into the season. Davis and Baker probably thought the same.

To put everything into context, since beating Accrington, the Alex had lost three and drawn two, scoring three and conceding thirteen. It was bloody awful form! The two previous games had been nothing short of embarrassing, losing 0-3 and 0-4. Why anyone expected anything less than defeat is beyond me. But what happened next tipped even some of the staunchest Davis supporters over the edge. It was a thrashing that left a dejected Crewe contingent wondering which way to turn. There had been many low points across the club's history, but losing 0-4 to an outfit relatively new to the Football League was shameful. It was a mess; three goals conceded either side of the half-time interval, with a fourth for good measure from one of the Fleetwood substitutes towards the end. Crewe fans not dependent upon coach travel had long since left the Highbury Stadium.

In reality, the Alex probably fielded a team earning less money than their opponents. Paying hefty wages never guarantees success, but it allows for strength in depth and the chance to attract players with considerable experience. Fleetwood had a rich and ambitious chairman prepared to pump his millions into the club. There was a revamped stadium, growing fan base and multiple promotions up the football pyramid under their belt. They were "doing" a Wimbledon, full of confidence and not scared of anyone. It was mission impossible for Crewe when the first goal hit the back of the net.

Some critical questions now needed to be asked. Top of the list was whether certain players were giving, say, 90% and taking things too easy? Okay, so dropping 10% sounds so trivial, and yet as part of a team that must fire on all cylinders it can be the weak link. Supporters forgive many things, but a lack of effort in club colours is the most heinous of football crimes. For the manager of any club it is a tricky situation. He cannot (indeed, should not) come out in public and point the finger at one or more individuals. That runs the risk of enraging supporters loyal to those players. Even the dressing room could erupt, the leaders jumping to the defence of their colleagues. It's a challenging task; but it's what the most successful managers are capable of. They have to, else they fail.

Davis was never likely to give in, or crumble under the pressure. He'd spent two decades in dressing rooms as a player, often as the captain. He was a winner, and his interviews with the press remained largely upbeat and bullish. The players needed to 'go back to basics with the defending' he told *The Crewe Chronicle*. 'We have to stop taking unnecessary risks and play safe. We have to mark better and make better decisions.' He didn't blame match officials or bemoan bad luck. It was always "we" he spoke of - the team, and the club. Despite several shocking scorelines, he believed that they were close to getting it right. Now he urgently needed to address the errors that cost them dear each week.

So assessing the next fixture must have made Davis weep. It was a trip to Preston, a strong side that had won four and drawn one of their last five. The trek up the M6 was a day out, no more. Supporters would enjoy a few beers to avoid Saturday shopping; there was just the football to interrupt an otherwise pleasant trip. Taking a point was highly unlikely.

UNBELIEVABLE!

So surprising the Lilywhites 2-0 on their own patch was nothing short of miraculous. Davis remained loyal to his beleaguered back four, and refused to shuffle his defence. That had raised plenty of eyebrows. Instead, he tweaked his strike options, returning Inman to an attacking/ midfield position. The former Newcastle United man repaid his gaffer with a vital goal that secured three precious points, adding to Moore's first-half effort. Aneke also starred, and hinted that he may yet find the consistency required to make it as a top player. At times he dazzled, easily beating his markers with skill and strength. The Deepdale crowd was speechless, as were many Alex fans.

And it got better, as Moore kept his cool in the 92nd minute at home to Bristol City the following week. He won the penalty, and with hearts in mouths a good Gresty Road crowd watched him out-fox the Robins' goalkeeper from the spot. One-nil, a clean sheet, and the kind of confidence-boost the players had needed since August. It nudged Crewe up to sixteenth in the table; vital breathing space and pressure off the manager - briefly!

Walking away from the ground that evening was a pleasure. There was a feeling of elation, incredible relief that we had won back-to-back games. It went further than that for me. Memories of Steve Holland flooded back, when his time in the hot seat looked increasingly unsecure. Any victory back then - like the 1-0 FA Cup win over Ebbsfleet (November 2008) during Holland's darkest period - sparked celebrations and instilled hope that he and Crewe Alexandra would find the magic formula. Most (and I mean that, upwards of 95%) DID NOT want Holland to fail, and nor did the core support want to see Davis flop during the difficult phase of October 2013. Everything hinged on the old adage that results count for everything. Now there was something to build on.

BOOM!

The expected momentum evaporated three days later. Stevenage destroyed Crewe in a ten-minute goal blitz. Even the Dugdale-Ellis partnership that many supporters had demanded looked wobbly. Mistake after mistake gifted the rampant visitors too many chances. The Alex defence could not cope, but the midfield was almost non-existent. They huffed and puffed, tackled and ran - in theory everything supporters insist upon. But they were hapless, ineffectual and lightweight. They exposed the back four too often. The game was lost before 8:15pm that Tuesday evening.

Davis was visibly shaken after the match and decided that now was the right time to be critical. 'We haven't been able to come from behind in any game; we haven't shown the fighting character. It is very disappointing because it was against a team which is down there and it would have helped us climb the table.' He didn't pick out specific players but it was blatantly obvious that he wanted more from certain individuals.

Against Sheffield United, however, there was the "fight" the manager needed from his team, but the same basic errors left the Alex once again chasing the game. Lee Molyneux, Mark Ellis, Liam Nolan and Chuks Aneke were dropped to the bench in a raft of changes. It was disappointing to see Aneke omitted but, after a good showing at Preston, he obviously had not done enough for the overall team cause. That remained crucial to any progress up the league.

The new-look side forced the Blades to work hard for possession. It was Nigel Clough's first match in charge. United had themselves hovered around the foot of the division all season, eventually forcing their board of directors to change manager. In many ways it was a fixture that Crewe should have targeted for at least a point, but Clough also wanted to make an impact. He needed to lift "his" crowd and revitalise the once-mighty club. Ultimately, they didn't really need to break sweat, as stupid mistakes and poor communication allowed them to punish us.

Thankfully, there was spirit and determination in what the Alex tried to achieve. Even at 0-3 down the players wanted something from the game, and when Clayton pulled one back after 77 minutes every supporter saw it as a lifeline rather than a consolation. That never-say-die attitude permeated from team to terrace and back. Davis and Baker barked it from the technical area, players yelled and fans roared. But it wasn't enough; Sheffield had sufficient steel to ride it out against the resurgent Alex. We could not stop the flow of goals conceded. It was another game lost. For the first time that season the Alex slipped into the bottom four. We had the worst defensive record of any of the 92 league clubs.

TIME TO GO!

The reaction on Sunday morning was expected. The Internet message boards were dominated by anti-Davis posts. By then the result had sunk in. Dejection had become anger. Everyone was hurting. Days later the voice of Rob Dutton, writing in *The Crewe Chronicle* under the Crewe Alexandra Supporters' Initiative banner, called for perspective. Asking whether 'the success under Davis' had led to 'such high expectations for the club' was a fair question. And he was right. Too many got carried away and reacted hastily. It was so easy to forget what progress had occurred under the latest incumbent. Dutton urged supporters not to panic or call for change, as Davis and Baker would 'do the business' necessary to correct things, he maintained.

Within days, they duly delivered. In came George Evans from Manchester City; a creative midfielder not afraid of a meaty challenge. Davis had his eye on others; a goalkeeper and another striker. But they could wait. Too many changes could unsettle the side further. He did not have the luxury of time, certainly not long enough to bed new players into his system. So in Evans went, against Bradford City who arrived at Crewe looking for (and needing) points themselves.

It was a turgid affair. There was little quality and few clear-cut chances in front of goal. Both sides were desperate to avoid defeat. They did, squeezing a 0-0 result that did little to inspire. The Alex strikers again fired blanks.

There are times when a distraction from league action is most welcome; when injuries have ravaged the side, or when several suspensions have kicked in. But when there is a chance of progress it can be a real hindrance. It was still shaky form, but after the Bradford draw the Alex boasted (if that is the right word) just two defeats in five league games. It was an improving trend!

So the start of the FA Cup came at the wrong time for Crewe. It wasn't even the most attractive of opening round draws - away at Wycombe. Adams Park is one of those okay but largely uninspiring grounds. It is set in idyllic surrounds, but for those out for a few beers it is a long way from the town centre. And yet it's friendly. In fact, Wycombe were one of the first clubs to start a new trend. Sheets of paper printed with "Welcome Crewe fans" were attached to the turnstile entrance and near catering facilities. How quaint! But therein lies one of the problems; it has never been a hotbed of football. Passions do not boil over on matchday. So visiting fans exchange pleasantries with the locals and everyone gets on with their business.

The game couldn't have started much better for Davis and his players. During the week, training had concentrated on shooting practice. It paid off, but not for the Alex forwards. Instead, Grant thumped a cracking 25-yarder past the Wycombe goalkeeper when the game was just four minutes old. That was it for Crewe, as Aneke, Moore and Clayton all fired high and wide with feeble efforts across the match. The hosts levelled before the break, and of the two sides they looked the more likely to progress. In many ways, it would have suited Crewe to ditch out early, giving everyone the chance to concentrate on all-important league matters. It was now two years since Davis had taken charge, and his successful stint as manager was looking bleaker by the day. He did not want relegation on his CV.

Perhaps taking a week off was the worst thing that could have happened, and maybe dropping to Wycombe's level lulled Davis et al into a false sense of security. Next up was Brentford at Griffin Park, table-toppers and looking likely to sustain the pace alongside Wolves. A goal either side of half time, and then three more towards the end of the game highlighted the gulf in class, ability and desire. Former Alex hitman Clayton Donaldson bagged two and Alex fans realised that a season of struggle was now a certainty. This was yo-yo football; up, down, briefly up again, and then down to rock bottom. We were not enjoying the ride. In fact, a very hostile group of about twenty Alex supporters let Davis and the players know exactly what they thought. They were beyond angry. Their comments cannot be repeated here!

Supporters can accept defeat when they appreciate the facts, when they know that the management has done everything possible to achieve the best result for their club. Any loss hurts like hell. You take it into the working week and can't shake it off until the next match day. But when the odds are stacked against you, there's a willingness to forgive. Although it was a painful experience, Brentford was one such scenario. The north London club were geared up for promotion to the Championship; every Alex fan knew that. They had a substantial wage bill, the pull of the capital city and a fan base larger than Crewe's. Unless a financial benefactor steps in at Gresty Road, beating teams like Brentford in the current climate is unlikely. That's still tough to accept, as we have leap-frogged the Bees in the past (no Crewe supporter will ever forget Shaun Smith's goal at Wembley '97, or indeed his strike from the halfway line at Griffin Park in the same season).

The same applies to Sheffield United. Although they had been in the doldrums, few expected even a point at Bramall Lane. It doesn't make accepting defeat much easier, but the players and manager are at least cut a little slack.

Losing to some clubs, however, is unacceptable; even in the eyes of the most rational fan sat in the stand. Wycombe from League Two slot into that bracket. They were a division beneath Crewe, and with a lower budget. No excuses. Plus it was round one of the FA Cup; in fact, this was the replay staged at Gresty Road three days after the Brentford collapse. It was the perfect opportunity to gain confidence; it was the chance to finish the job. Watching that second-round draw would bring light relief and the chance of adventure. So to lose 0-2 at home against the Chairboys was the ultimate kick in the ribs. It was freezing, and the crowd of just 1,695 hinted at a long, hard winter ahead. We offered barely anything across ninety dull minutes. The highlights, in fact the only moments of real excitement, were second half goals by the visitors. A sarcastic cheer greeted the "winner" that ended our FA Cup journey for another season. In reality, it was no contest. The Alex never looked like scoring.

DESPONDENT!

'This is a low as it gets. We have let the fans down big-style tonight. I am very disappointed. I expected so much better. They deserved to go through and we deserved what we got,' was the manager's reaction and veiled apology to supporters.

I didn't join the booing that dominated the final whistle that evening, but the frustration on supporters' faces was all-too evident. Many were concerned that the team were going backwards. After such incredible success nobody wanted to throw it all away. Consolation the previous season seemed so long ago. The backlash was in full swing. If ever the manager needed a lift it was now.

SAY HELLO, WAVE GOODBYE...

The first third of the 2013/14 season was a car crash. There is no other way of wrapping it up. If something could go wrong, it did. What became increasingly apparent, however, was that the nonsense at Cornwall, alleged player fall-outs and injuries were not the only reasons for our shocking form. The players were still trying, giving 100% in most cases. But there was something missing. Rebalancing the team after yet another high-profile sale was nigh-on impossible. There was no tailor-made replacement for Luke Murphy. It was unrealistic to think that like-for-like could be bought in, and although loan players would help they were unlikely to be experienced or capable of matching Murphy's vision.

The flow of player sales has become increasingly problematic at Crewe, especially since Steve Davis took over. That's not down to him, rather the financial hardships faced by everyone - including football clubs. I refer in particular to the last four or five years (2009-14). The club has raised considerable sums of cash, but key players have been ripped from the team's core. It's not necessarily about failed relationships (as per the *Soft Cell* song "Say hello, wave goodbye" of the early 1980s), although some might say that a young player refusing to sign a new deal is evidence that something has gone sour. But any breakup or departure often leaves one party wounded. That is usually us; the fans. One moment those players are bursting onto the Alex scene; the next we are watching them step out for Championship and Premiership clubs on TV. Too often these days there doesn't seem to be much in between.

Murphy's exit wasn't badly timed, but the combined fall-out from his, Powell and Westwood's departure was too-much, too-soon. We'll focus on the midfield duo later, but Powell's high-profile sale to Manchester United left fans short-changed. For me, he undoubtedly moved too soon. Sure he made a considerable contribution to that promotion cause, and flicking through some of the many YouTube clips it's apparent how many exceptional goals he scored between November 2011 and May 2012. But is that enough in the grand scheme of things? Aside from the club's bank manager breathing easier, is 64 appearances really good value for Crewe supporters? Only 55 of those were in the league, and 21 were as a substitute. So Powell only started 34 league games for Crewe Alexandra. That startled me when I checked it out.

The feeling that fans are somehow cheated by players leaving prematurely is something that has troubled me for many years. Maybe "cheated" is the wrong word; rankled would be more appropriate. The landscape, however, has changed considerably. Cast your minds back to 1988, when a young David Platt moved on to Aston Villa for £200,000. Crewe fans were elated. The club banked decent money, certainly the first big cash injection since I'd become an Alex supporter in the mid-1970s. Apart from a few quid for Gary Blissett (£60,000 in 1986), Steve Davis (£15,000 in 1987) and Geoff Thomas (£50,000 in 1987), we'd never been what you'd call a selling club. Players arrived, then got released, walked away or retired.

So the Platt sale put Dario Gradi and Gresty Road on the map. It was a significant step up for a Division Four [League Two these days] footballer. Platt was talented, and like Nick Powell during the 2011/12 season, he stood out from the journeymen around him in the 1987/88 season. By way of comparison, Platt spent three full seasons at Gresty Road, made 134 league appearances and scored 54 goals. That, in my opinion, is value for money for the supporters. Gradi took Platt straight from Manchester United, invested time and effort helping to hone his skills, and helped turn him into an England star. We watched visionary passing and some great goals; I am sure that others prospered because of him. Platt was gone before the successful 1988/89 promotion season concluded, but he helped to sow the seeds.

MURPHY'S PIGEON!

To see how the player sales evolved at Crewe, we must skip forward a decade from the Platty era. A good starting point would be Danny Murphy. Now a TV pundit in his mid-thirties, Murph announced himself to Crewe fans in late 1993. Across that inaugural season he was used sparingly as a substitute. As a 17-year-old he made his mark. He became a first-team regular and started to gel with formidable striker Dele Adebola and fellow midfielder Gareth Whalley. But it was Murphy's last two seasons that Alex fans will recall fondly.

In 1995/96 he hit the target frequently, but in his final campaign (1996/97) he missed just one game and scored an incredible 15 goals, giving centre-forward Adebola a run for his money. At Wembley, before his move to Anfield in July 1997 (for £3,000,000), he delivered the cross that led to the winning play-off goal against Brentford. Nobody begrudged him the move to Liverpool, his boyhood club. Murphy played 132 league games for the Alex and scored 27 goals (he later returned on loan, making 16 further appearances and scoring one goal). Oh, and that transfer fee would equate to roughly £5m if you factor in inflation over 15 years. He served his time and made the club a packet, and who can forget the fabulous "Murphy had a pigeon" song!

DEANO!

Next up is Dean Ashton. He broke the Alex mould. While diminutive midfielders were Gradi's signature dish, Ashton added a new dimension to the Gresty Road menu. He was a monster, but he also had the touch, the vision and a scary nose for goal. At 6'2" and nearly thirteen stone Deano cut an imposing figure. When he moved on to Norwich (for £3,000,000 in January 2005) many said it was too soon, that his departure ruined any chance of us grabbing a play-off spot. At the time, we'd enjoyed a cracking run and sat tenth in the Championship. We beat Leeds United 2-0 at Elland Road on New Year's Day. We all got carried away.

Then we lost our talisman striker. The Alex didn't win any of the next 19 games. In perhaps the most dramatic and desperate end-of-season finales, we beat Coventry on the last day to stay in the division. Selling Ashton was, many cried, a huge error on the part of the club. But any criticism of his sale was unfounded. Deano was ready for a fresh challenge. He was too good for the second tier. Many supporters called for Gradi and the board to strengthen the attack, to replace the free-scoring striker. That was ludicrous. He was unique.

So where does this lead us? Those examples (Platt, Murphy and Ashton) highlight two things: several years' service and significant league appearances. Nobody, in my opinion, could or should suggest that either the players or club did not benefit from their contributions or transfer fees received.

Let us wind forward and assess two of the most recent departures (for good money), and consider one "potential" exit that could invoke a wholly different source of remuneration.

First, Nicky Maynard: yet another Cheshire-born lad, he debuted as an 18-year-old at home to Millwall on the final day of the 2005/06 season. And he scored, with his first touch! We rubbed our hands and looked forward to the following campaign. Maynard had pace, a wicked shot and knew how to beat a 'keeper. And he hit the ground running. He racked up 38 appearances and scored 19 goals across the 2006/07 season; impressive. That was Gradi's last season (well, prior to the first handover) before Steve Holland took charge.

Things went pear-shaped for Maynard (and Crewe) after the first game of the 2007/08 season. The Alex beat Brighton but Maynard broke his leg and damaged ankle ligaments. He didn't get back to full fitness and goal-scoring prowess until the following February. Then he went goal-crazy, hitting thirteen in eleven games. And then he was gone, to Bristol City for £2,250,000 in July 2008.

By my reckoning, we got one and a half seasons from Maynard. We fixed him up after his injury, got him back on track, enjoyed some great goals but then watched him fly the nest. He was 21 years old when he moved to Ashton Gate. It was far too soon in my opinion. He owed us another season.

Now, let's move on to the first major export following the 2012 promotion: Nick Powell. Was this and later transactions likely to prove confrontational at Crewe? My line of thought involves Davis, and the man who set the academy wheels in motion, Gradi. With new roles defined, is there a conflict of interests? It's an oddity largely unique to Crewe Alexandra. The academy costs in excess of £1m to run each year, but also feeds the first team (some of expenditure is covered by football grants, but the club must find around £700,000 each season to sustain the Reaseheath production line). We need those youth products to excel so that they yield big bucks.

The fact that our players prosper and move on to great things helps to sell the concept to parents keen to find the best footballing nursery for their kids. But supporters see big-money deals sealed and wonder why the club does not invest immediately in replacements on the pitch. It doesn't work like that. The profits fuel the next phase of academy development. And so on…

While Davis is fully supportive of the Alex ethos, and allowing players to move on is an essential part of the club's business model, it must give him sleepless nights. Gradi, meanwhile, always has put the footballers' best interests first. Seeing Powell move on to one of the country's top teams must have filled him with pride. That's what the Alex youth system is all about. The transaction made the club a fistful of dollars; Powell helped secure us promotion and added to Gradi's illustrious CV. We shouldn't grumble, but it doesn't sit right with me.

Money aside, the end result wreaked havoc with the manager's plans for the 2012/13 campaign. Powell's departure was a given, and yet many of us held out faint hopes that he might start the new season, or return on loan as part of any deal. As a supporter, I would have liked to see him operate in League One. Who knows what could have happened? I want Crewe Alexandra as a whole to prosper; not just individual players. Instead, Davis and the Alex stepped up a level, lost perhaps the best player and we were up against it from day one.

Of course, the situation deteriorated further for Davis just months after Powell was whisked away. It was unusual, but a second deal was completed.

DOUBLE-WHAMMY!

Ashley Westwood was snapped up by Aston Villa. He rose through the academy system and earned his first team stripes at the tail-end of the 2008/09 season under Gudjon Thordarson. Across the next three full seasons he was pivotal to the side, and rarely missed a game. When he did, it was often as he served a suspension following an over-exuberant challenge. He never backed out of a tackle. He improved slowly and became the midfield conductor of most incisive moves into opposition territory. There was also a steady flow of goals. He was the archetypal all-rounder.

As rumours of a move filtered through at the start of the 2012/13 season (initially it was interest from Swansea), Westwood had amassed 134 league appearances. He played just four games in August 2012, and then completed his move to Villa (£2,000,000). I do not think anyone can have any complaints about his contribution to the Alex cause, but he left another gaping hole in the midfield - and when the new season had already started. I know that it's a complex equation, balancing expectations, money matters and what's best for the club, but I think the Westwood deal ticked every box. It just left us short, and the timing was awful.

The Alex did adjust to life after Powell/Westwood but largely because of one man: Luke Murphy. He emerged alongside them and was already a first-team regular when they moved on. Although it stretched him and the overall game plan, he kept things ticking over. He scored goals, fed the strikers and was a superb buffer in front of the back four. Still, we did well to consolidate that season, and lifting the JPT was enough to distract from growing problems.

***

For the purposes of this book we must come bang up to date. The new manager enjoyed stunning success in a relatively short space of time, but immediately faced monumental challenges. Within just twelve months, Davis was forced to oversee the exit of three key men. Not only were they talented individuals, they were players that made the whole side tick. Midfield men (with outrageous attacking flair and a prolific nose for goal in Powell's case) that instigated virtually every move, controlled play, kept possession and pressed the opposition into submission. Now that sounds flowery and completely exaggerated, but it's not.

For Crewe Alexandra, Davis and the fans, that collective departure was hugely significant. Here, for the statistically minded amongst you, are a few facts and figures (league games only):

From November 2011, when Davis took over, through to May 2012, the Alex won 14 (48%), drew 11 (38%) and lost 4 (14%). During that time, they scored 48 and conceded 32 goals (+16 GD). That team included Powell, Westwood and Murphy. As this was a reduced season in terms of statistics directly relevant to Davis (29 games post-Gradi), I have included the won-drawn-lost totals as percentages. It makes it far easier comparing like-for-like over the next two seasons.

For 2012/13 season, after the two sales (although Westwood did start the season): won 18 (39%), drew 10 (22%) and lost 18 (39%). We scored 54 and conceded 62 (-8 GD).

For 2013/14 season, with Murphy now gone: won 13 (28%), drew 12 (26%) and lost 21 (46%). We scored 54 and conceded 77 (-23 GD).

There is an obvious trend, but take a closer look at the drilled-down season data and there's another pattern. The immediate period after the sales was horrendous, and the Alex won once during the first ten games of both campaigns. We struggled to adjust after Powell/Westwood moved on and very much so after Murphy departed. The bought-in players did not fill the gaps. There was an urgent need to bring in loan players, as it was asking far too much for youngsters like Billy Waters, Liam Nolan and Ollie Turton to make the transition quickly.

The most alarming statistic is the goals conceded. For me it highlights not just the defensive qualities of Westwood and Murphy in particular, but the fact that in any given game they retained possession. That in turn meant that the opposition could not attack our defence. To further justify that theory across 2012-2014, the same six defenders were deployed: Kelvin Mellor, Mark Ellis, Adam Dugdale, Harry Davis, George Ray and Matt Tootle. They were young players, gaining experience and improving. They did not become inept overnight. After all, that Mellor-Ellis-Davis-Tootle combination kept a clean sheet at Wembley when the side beat Southend to lift the JPT! Ultimately, they missed a reliable figure positioned just in front of the back four. They became increasingly exposed and their mistakes were magnified.

Moving forward I worry that the pressure to sell will only increase. The Football League has tried to stamp out financial bad practice, linking wages to turnover and insisting that creditors are paid before transfer bans are lifted. Those restrictions will become more severe, squeezing clubs further to avoid the bankruptcies that have blighted the game. That's fair enough, as the urge to stretch and chase success is a recipe for disaster for the smaller clubs.

Alex chairman John Bowler never did that. He fought tirelessly to keep the club in good health, but the only way to balance our books has been to cash in on talent. Gate receipts and matchday sales are insufficient to keep Crewe Alexandra afloat; that's a frightening thought when you consider that we have been run on a tightly-controlled budget. Others are reckless.

Gradi, too, was always on board and strove to keep the Alex solvent; he appreciated that player sales were essential. If Powell, Westwood and Murphy had not emerged and attracted the big clubs, there is every chance that the Alex would have gone under. That's the harsh reality. It was that close.

TOO MUCH, TOO SOON!

But surely there comes a break point, where we have allowed too many players to move on and where too much is invested in youth at the academy? That's when the financial return does not compensate for the turmoil created to the matchday squad. I believe this happened after the summer of 2013 and so nearly undid the great work done since Davis took over. Gradi and the academy were fine, several million pounds banked to ensure that the Reaseheath operation prospered over several more seasons. But the front line punters nearly watched "our" team slide back into the basement division.

The other key factor is the fast-changing attitude of players. Youngsters progressing from academies to first teams now know that securing their financial future is possible in a few short years. They watch the elite earning hundreds of thousands of pounds every week and dream of achieving similar themselves. At Crewe only modest riches are on offer, but when you see players go direct to Aston Villa and Manchester United, it is no surprise that the up-and-coming talent wants the same.

The problem is players from the same age group. With Nick Powell gone, his eighteen-year-old buddy Max Clayton appeared to have his eyes on a move. When Ashley Westwood secured his move, you can bet that Luke Murphy fancied his chances the following season. They weren't greedy, but they too wanted to see what the wider footballing world had to offer. The Alex could not, and would not, hold them to ransom. That would break club promises. The players now have the power. It is a monster of our own creation.

There is no simple answer. These days, when a player wants to move on it's just a question of when, not if the deal happens. Even in the top flight, the players hold the cards. Agents trawl the markets constantly, and players know what is out there. It is often all about the cash. We cannot stop this trend, and yet I'd like to see academy players involved across three full seasons before a transfer can be considered. Perhaps a minimum number of appearances should be required, like fulfilling an apprenticeship and earning your stripes.

Deep down I know that imposing unrealistic restrictions on youngsters would not work. Players, agents, clubs and the governing leagues would all have to sign up. That will never happen. So the compensation route is in place to soften the blow. Clubs are rewarded for the efforts invested in the academy players and receive financial reward based on several factors - time served, plus appearances and the level played at, for example.

**

Towards the end of the 2013/14 season, academy product Max Clayton delayed signing a new contract. That frustrated everyone; especially the manager who was left in limbo not knowing if the player would be part of his pre-season plans in July. At the time of writing (June 2014), the situation had not been resolved. Clayton had served the club well. He had been involved since he was a young boy. Now he was in the driving seat. The club had to wait, hoping that he would trust them and continue his development at Gresty Road.

The situation could be repeated. In the future, if an academy player has a contract offer on the table and does choose to move on, then Crewe will receive a decent sum. Unfortunately, it will be nothing like the player's true worth. For the Alex to receive substantial transfer fees, the players concerned need to cement a regular first-team place. They need to perform, score goals and attract the attention of the biggest clubs. That is what Powell, Westwood and Murphy did. Clayton showed flashes of brilliance, but an injury set him back. When he returned his form was decent, but his overall game lacked goals.

Perhaps his patience ran out? Maybe the lad just fancied spreading his wings? I would like to think that the Crewe "kids" move on for the right reasons; not for money alone. But maybe that is far too romantic a notion.

The reality is that many League Two and most League One clubs pay higher wages than Crewe. And where football has become no more than a job to some, they are always likely to take the fattest pay cheque. My worry is that more of our graduates will follow this pattern, with the youngsters wanting quicker moves that yield the kind of pay that the Alex cannot offer. We could become dependent on tribunal fees.

***

Luke Murphy was never egotistical or presumptuous about his move; but it was his time. He saw the links and heard the rumours just as we did. It was coming. Davis and Baker knew how much he'd be missed, but it was impossible to react until the sale became reality. When he finally waved goodbye it was too late to recruit. There were good prospects in the U21 age group but none of Murphy or Westwood's calibre.

Talking to the management duo soon after Murphy's sale they were candid. They told me it was going to be hard. Before a ball was kicked ahead of the 2013/14 roller-coaster they knew it was more likely to be about relegation than further consolidation. His departure did not cause ripples, it more a tsunami. Davis needed to batten down the hatches and find calm waters before he could plot a way out of the mire.

As yet another aside, I'll end this chapter with a comparison. At the end of the 2013/14 season Southampton finished eighth in the Premier League. They were in the top half of the division all season and peaked at third in October 2013. The Saints boast crowds of around 30,000 and a number of their players perform at international level. That, however, does not mean that they can hang onto their stars - or, indeed, their manager! As the dust settled and the nation geared up for the 2014 World Cup in Brazil, Mauricio Pochettino quit the St. Mary's Stadium after just 18 months to become manager at Tottenham Hotspur.

The first team was also set to be decimated. Striker Ricky Lambert signed for Liverpool, and Luke Shaw, Adam Lallana and Jay Rodriguez looked set to join other clubs later in the summer. Roll back a few seasons and other high-profile performers like Gareth Bale (Tottenham and now

Real Madrid), Theo Walcott and Oxlade Chamberlain (both Arsenal) moved on before Saints fans had chance to see them blossom. Like the Crewe set-up at Reaseheath, the Southampton academy has been producing excellent young players for many years. If ever a club needed a loyal servant like Matthew Le Tissier it was Southampton! We moan at Gresty Road, but imagine how Southampton supporters must feel? Even the top clubs have to sell.

The south coast club can at least console themselves with the considerable fees and compensation received for their key assets. They will buy, strengthen and also recruit another proven manager. At Crewe there were no such millions available for rebuilding. Davis, Baker, Bowler et al have to work within their means and get on with it.

The 2013/14 season was about to get very serious...

FALSE DAWN

Friday 22nd November 2013 was a good day at Crewe Alexandra. I say "good" in that seven players received news that the Cornwall allegations would be taken no further. There would be no prosecutions, and no court appearances to disrupt an already chaotic season. 'All seven men have been released without any action being taken against them,' Devon and Cornwall Police confirmed.

My first reaction was relief, but for entirely selfish reasons. The football, I thought, could now get back to normal. There was a similar reaction from everyone I spoke with across the day. I had to check myself, think beyond the headlines that would be splashed on the Internet and across the front page of the next issues of *The Crewe Chronicle* and *The Crewe & Nantwich Guardian*. What about the woman? Whatever happened that night/early morning in July she and her family would now be feeling awful, wouldn't they? If the men from Crewe had not been charged, where did that leave her?

MUD STICKS!

There were certainly no winners from the sorry incident that had stretched across four months. In addition to the police investigation, a number of Alex fans had gladly pointed the finger, suggesting that something must have happened. For some the player-supporter relationship was badly damaged. In fact, I heard about some fans that had boycotted games from the start of the season. They were disgusted and refused to attend matches until the case was resolved. I suppose we can only rely upon the British justice system, but even in the days following the "good news" the saga did not sit well with me.

One thing was for sure: the Alex were in a mess. With its players cleared, the club needed to get back to winning ways. That wasn't going to be easy, as the next visitors to Gresty Road were Port Vale. What an opportunity, though, to re-launch the season; a feisty local derby to set hearts racing for the right reasons!

Unfortunately the statistics did not make pleasant reading. Just to recap, before the Vale match, of the 21 league and cup games played since August, the Alex had lost twelve of them. We had won just four matches, and one of those was a first round 1-0 grind over Accrington Stanley in the Johnstone's Paint Trophy. That's a horrendous sequence by anyone's standards.

Incredibly, ahead of the match, Steve Davis was forced to confront another potentially explosive issue. When the team sheets emerged there were two names missing, not just from the starting XI but from the matchday squad. Anthony Grant and Bradden Inman were excluded. The details were patchy, but before we had left the Brunswick, everyone was talking about player bust-ups and bad attitudes.

The other change was the addition of Neil Etheridge, a 23-year-old 'keeper signed on loan from Fulham. The Alex had conceded far too many goals already, and many had looked to young Ben Garratt and his inexperience as the prime reason. That was harsh, as the lad was bedding in as best he could. The Fulham loanee, however, set tongues wagging. Not for the single appearance he had made for the west London club, but for his bizarre international pedigree. Although he'd struggled to break into the Premiership with his host club, he already boasted forty two appearances for the Philippines.

With Max Clayton ruled out through injury, it was a much-changed team from the lame FA Cup defeat to Wycombe. There were obvious concerns, and we all wondered if the revamped line-up would settle sufficiently to cope with Port Vale. We applauded, cheered the names as they were read out, and then watched the game burst into life below us.

What happened out on the pitch heartened even the greatest cynics. There was a zest about Crewe's play, the football was considered and promised an end product. Most important, there was an obvious togetherness about the team.

We even took the lead, a tidy strike from George Evans who was on loan from Man City. When he scored, perhaps ten minutes before half time, the Alex players went crazy. It was as though someone had popped a champagne cork, releasing weeks if not months of pent up frustration and pressure. The whole side seemed to pile on the loanee midfielder, every man desperate to celebrate the goal.

The home crowd soared. For the first time in over a month the Alex were winning a league game. This was it; surely it was set to be our day? This was the turning point, the defining moment of a miserable season.

AJ Leitch-Smith fizzed, slipping past the Vale defenders with a renewed spring in his step. He fed Byron Moore who suddenly looked alive again. Both could play, and both knew how to put the ball away; they had the Alex running through their veins. The second killer goal was imminent. It had to be. The Alex always needed more than one.

It didn't happen, at least not for the Alex. Vale equalised and we all slumped back into our seats as the half-time whistle sounded. And yet there was hope in everyone's heart, and over beers, coffee and pies. There was excitement ahead of the second period, and the Alex looked determined. They wanted to win. We were up for it!

That desire was evident straight after the break. Leitch-Smith could have scored, and then Moore blasted over from close range. That should have sealed it for Crewe, but it wasn't to be. Etheridge was called upon increasingly, and the game was played out almost entirely in the Alex half as the clock wound down.

DAMN!

The one man always likely to be involved on his Crewe return did the damage. Tom Pope roughed up anyone in his path, fought toe-to-toe and flicked on a cross for Vale's Jennison Myrie-Williams to tap home at the back post. Vale had won it. Deflated doesn't begin to sum up how we felt. For some time our group stood there, speechless and shell-shocked. We had deserved much more than a point and yet ended the night empty handed.

The only crumb of comfort was watching a Vale idiot unceremoniously hauled from the ground for jumping onto the pitch. It was another defeat. We had taken two points from fifteen. And yet there was no moaning; the groans and gasps on the final whistle had been ever hopeful that we would rescue another point. There was no negativity, no boos or frustrated chanting. It was as though the club as a whole had been lifted, on and off the pitch, and everyone was ready and willing to march forward together.

That new-found camaraderie was evident after the match. I traded the usual banter on forums, Twitter and Facebook during the following hours. Defender Matt Tootle used Twitter to tell the Alex fans (and, indeed, the world) exactly what he thought. It made great reading. He talked of "fight" and keeping the fans "behind us" and, crucially, signed off with a hashtag (a word or phrase that links topics on Twitter) that told us all to #believe.

Tootle also referenced that they had been "a team again", and that went a long way towards explaining why certain players had been omitted from the side that day. This was the new talking point. It had been yet another major issue for the beleaguered manager to deal with, just hours after the Cornwall cloud had lifted. It never rains, it pours!

Grant and Inman had, apparently, let the manager down. Their attitude had been poor and they had unsettled some of the younger squad members. Davis threw a little psychology into the mix and announced that it would be up to the other players if the rogue pair was to be allowed back into training. Good old-fashioned peer pressure would sort it out. Supporters watched on as Davis regained control. That was reassuring, and for the first time in ages I felt as though the anti-Davis camp backed off. It felt strange that another defeat had galvanised the team and fans, but we still needed the results to improve.

It would have been perfect if the turnaround was completed a few days later at Brunton Park. But at Carlisle the season was summed up in one bicycle kick. Vadaine Oliver, still struggling to secure a regular starting position, played the full ninety minutes. During a cracking spell for the Alex, he took a looping cross in his stride and converted with his back to goal. It was spectacular. It deserved to give us the lead. It was disallowed. Carlisle hit two quick goals before the break. The new-found belief drained away, and Carlisle went on to win 2-1. We had lost two more games. It had been a false dawn.

The next three weeks proved almost as testing. During that period there was also a break, a match-free weekend while others enjoyed the FA Cup second round. It gave Davis time to work with his players, analyse games, iron out mistakes and work out how to win again. As he prepared his squad to face Crawley at Gresty Road it was eight games since we had tasted victory.

I don't think that the pressure increased, as by now most had written the season off. It wasn't a foregone conclusion, but most saw our chances of survival as decidedly bleak. We were a permanent fixture in the bottom four places. It was the end of November and relegation was discussed. I did not accept that. But unless something miraculous happened before Christmas, everything pointed to a scrap to avoid the drop being our only source of excitement in the latter stages of the season.

AT LAST!

Beating Crawley offered much encouragement, but it came at a price. First, Vadaine Oliver's bad luck continued. He was harshly booked just after half-time for catching his opponent with his arm as both men jumped for the ball. Minutes later, when the Gresty Road crowd watched Oliver felled in the area everyone screamed for a penalty. The referee blew his whistle but gave the Crewe striker a second yellow card for diving. There was uproar. It was a clear foul. Davis and the players were still remonstrating as Oliver walked to the dressing room.

That kind of decision knocks the stuffing out of a team. It was as though nothing was going to go our way. Another defeat looked on the cards as the visitors stepped up the pressure. Davis reshuffled, and eventually threw Chuks Aneke into the action. He replaced Tom Hitchcock, on loan from QPR. The Alex squad that day included five loan players. The manager was exploring every avenue, looking beyond the young players who had taken a psychological knock following the painful start to the season. He needed pace, muscle and a little Premiership quality to lift the players who had dropped their heads. Aneke brought all that to the table. He mixed things up as soon as he raced into the action. His first significant contribution was to latch onto Matt Tootle's floated cross. The Arsenal lad stooped low and planted a firm header beyond the Crawley goalkeeper.

GOAL!

And what relief! The stadium rocked to a collective outpouring of emotion. We deserved it. The referee had wronged us. Oliver must have punched their air as he sat wallowing in his early bath. Now the Alex just had to ride out the final minutes with ten men. They did, with Aneke going close again before Crawley's Andy Drury left everyone holding their breath when his last-minute header sailed inches over the crossbar. One-nil, scrappy and fraught, but the first win in nine matches. It was a priceless result.

It was a start, nothing more. Speaking to *The Crewe Chronicle* ahead of the next match the Alex manager emphasised the size of the task ahead. 'We know we have got to be better during the second half of the season and we cannot just keep thinking that we have enough games to get out of trouble. We do have a lot of points to play for - we are not quite at halfway yet - but we have got to get ourselves out of the situation.'

It was no rousing speech but he let his players know that they had to rise to the task. It was asking too much to expect back-to-back wins, but a point away at Coventry from a 2-2 draw was a definite bonus. Under Steven Pressley, the Sky Blues had surged up the table and wiped out their 10-point deduction imposed after they were placed into administration. At Northampton's Sixfields stadium, Coventry's temporary home, Davis was again forced to make changes. Most significant was Ben Garratt who stepped in for the injured loanee goalkeeper Neil Etheridge. It was another blow, but also gave the Crewe youngster more vital match practice.

Although Garratt conceded twice, he completed the test with credit. His defenders were guilty of dithering for Coventry's first, and he was left exposed for the second. Callum Wilson raced clear of a static back four and Garratt was forced to challenge the forward. The penalty was inevitable and the Alex goalkeeper couldn't block the spot kick.

The bad luck didn't let up against Shrewsbury. For several minutes we all stood horrified as players, medics and stretcher-bearers rushed to Adam Dugdale's side. The fearless defender clashed heads and came off worst. It looked serious. The players were visibly shaken. Duggy had nearly swallowed his tongue. That forced an immediate change, and Mark Ellis was brought on as the ambulance arrived at the gates.

That's where the drama ended. A goal apiece, plenty of stupid errors, poor finishing by both teams along with a hatful of wasted opportunities, emphasised why both clubs were struggling at the wrong end of the division. The point was decent, but the best news of the afternoon came with confirmation that Dugdale had been released from Leighton Hospital.

Although the mini run was a massive boost, what we really needed was three points again - desperately. The two draws were not enough to lift us out of the drop zone. But there was now a sense of belief that we had a fighting chance.

What concerned me was the list of Alex goalscorers. It was unclear whether the loan players' temporary deals would be extended in January. The New Year threatened to be an uncomfortable ride if the club's own players could not find their shooting boots. We had become too reliant on Aneke and Hitchcock in particular.

The real pain came on Boxing Day. Nobody scored for Crewe and table-toppers Wolves bagged a relatively comfortable win; at least on paper. The reality was that Davis set his side up to contain Kenny Jackett's team and hit them on the break. Although we rode our luck, the plan almost worked.

The game started badly when Garratt had to pick the ball out of the net after just three minutes. The Wolves strikers looked rampant, too fast and powerful for the Alex back four. Wolves even kept £6m man Kevin Doyle on the bench. It looked set to be a long and arduous afternoon. It was a moment when many of the travelling fans wished that they had remained at home with relatives, picking over Christmas turkey and scoffing chocolates.

Thankfully, there was enough determination about the Crewe performance to keep Wolves pegged back. They became frustrated, and the 22,000 home supporters were restless when the game progressed without further goals for the men in gold. The Alex created chances, especially through Aneke who was progressing with each game, but the crucial difference between the teams was finishing. Wolves were clinical.

Most of their efforts hit the target, while Crewe shot high, wide and into bodies determined to keep a clean sheet.

Once again Davis utilised all three substitutes. The surprise was Anthony Grant. Just a few weeks after the "fall out" over his apparent bad attitude, the manager put faith in the combative midfielder once again. They seemed to have resolved their differences. Davis had confronted the issue head on. Now he had a valuable asset at his disposal. And Grant made a difference, tackling and harrying constantly.

The gulf in class was dramatically highlighted in the final minutes. Aneke gifted AJ Leitch-Smith a golden opportunity to return to the score sheet, but the Crewe-born lad tapped a pitiful effort wide. Had that gone in I believe that confidence would have rocketed. It would have been the ultimate catalyst, the springboard to launch the revival we all yearned for. By this stage it was all about belief, and that miss saw hearts sink. And Wolves delivered the hammer blow in stoppage time, giving our strikers a lesson in how to score. Scottish international Leigh Griffiths stole past two Alex players and cracked a thunderous shot past Garratt.

SUNK!

We didn't deserve that, but the top-notch finishing set Wolves apart. The hard work of the previous month was undone. It was a spirited performance but yielded no points. We hit rock bottom and sunk to the foot of the table. It felt as though we were swimming against the tide. The most dispiriting aspect of it all was that we came close. We matched one of the division's frontrunners. It counted for nothing. It was a miserable Christmas.

PETE

For me, the Alex staff, many of the club's supporters and several of my close friends, *She Wore A Scarlet Ribbon* was tinged with sadness as I recorded the passing of two great people. Chapters about Alex kit man John Fleet and supporter Mike Lazenby gave a sombre tone to the story of my journey with Mistress Alexandra. Unfortunately death is one of life's certainties that creeps up on us all, just far too soon for some. The football brought us all together, and at least the weekly dose of everything Alex makes sure that we will never forget them.

On Saturday 22nd February 2014, away at Vale Park, we won the match but lost another Alex stalwart. Pete Warburton was the official Crewe Alexandra photographer. His smiling face and considerable technical kit could be seen home and away, in rain or shine. He often wore his trademark cap. If you didn't know him, then he would often go unnoticed. Pete didn't make a fuss, demand attention or need people to know who he was or what he did.

Everyone reading these pages knew his work. His images filled the club's matchday program and graced publications and websites for the best part of a decade. The game against Port Vale was just another assignment, although his footballing passions were always with Crewe. Details of the match itself form part of this book's next chapter, but moments after the final whistle Pete's season and life ended all too suddenly.

The derby was a volatile affair. During the afternoon the Alex photographer took up a number of positions, recording a historical moment when three members of the Davis family took part in the same game (Steve, Harry and Joe of course), capturing the frantic match action, then snapping noisy, boisterous and - ultimately - delighted Alex supporters dancing and singing in the away enclosure.

On the final whistle he grabbed some fabulous pictures of the players and management coming over to the Crewe fans. It was a crazy celebration on the back of a fully deserved win, and to most of those going wild behind the goal, Pete was just another guy pointing his camera. And yet everyone posed, pointed and put on their best portrait face, because he encouraged that. He always nodded for approval before he clicked the shutter. It was an incredible day out and he was in the right place at the right time. I was sat about six rows from the front, and as usual he was beaming, ecstatic to see the Alex get three points and delighted at the mass of happy faces in front of him. We were his canvas and he painted with relish.

As we made our way out of the ground, dodging vicious comments and a few random missiles from disgruntled home supporters, Pete made his way to the official exit by the dugouts, about to mount the steps of the press box, taking a few more pictures no doubt. He was always on duty. But that's where he stopped, taken ill suddenly. Colleagues and officials rushed to help, but even with the quick action of medical staff it was too late.

Everyone leaving Burslem was oblivious to the tragedy until the first messages filtered onto the various social media sites. There was shock and disbelief, and I swapped messages with a couple of people to make sure there hadn't been a mistake. I didn't want to believe it, but the news slowly sunk in and what had been a joyful day became one of the saddest of the season.

I wouldn't describe Pete as a close friend, but he was someone I spoke with each and every time we caught each other's eye at matches. At the Wembley play-off final against Cheltenham he was busy grabbing pictures of fans excitedly awaiting kick-off; friends and family scattered across thousands of seats. He saw me chatting with a few mates and lowered his camera, waved, shouted "hello" and asked if we were enjoying ourselves. He did that to countless others. There were similar exchanges before, during and after so many Crewe games over recent seasons.

A game that sticks in my mind is a friendly against Nantwich Town in the summer of 2012. Alan Martin was in goal taking a few practice shots in his stride. Pete was snapping away and took up a position by the corner flag to grab the all-important angle of another save. He always did get the best perspective, using light perfectly to capture mood and moments like nobody else. I was hanging over the barrier and dropped a cheeky comment in his ear, trying to put him off his shot. It didn't work, of course, as he was the consummate professional. He chuckled, caught the action he needed, checked his result on the digital display, and looked around with an infectious smile. 'No chance, Hornbrook,' he told me. And then 'how are you?' without changing gear. That was Pete – friendly, affable and unflappable, professional and yet very personable.

Perhaps my first moment with the photographer was during a charity event driven by Crewe & Nantwich Borough Council, in the days before Cheshire East Council came into being. I was still updating the Crewe Blog website, a day-to-day words and photo diary of the town. I grabbed stories ad hoc, but also attended many of the formal press events that attracted *The Crewe Chronicle*, *Evening Sentinel*, local *Crewe*

Guardian, and also council press officers and freelance photographers like Pete. I stood side-by-side with him one day, brandishing my modest Canon camera and trying to get the light balance just right. He looked at me for a moment and then threw in a little advice. It was simple, straightforward stuff, the kind of information garnered over many years. While many craftsmen are sometimes guarded and keep trade secrets close to their chest, he was always happy to divulge handy tips. I saw him do similar to amateurs and professionals alike over the years. In the background, without wanting to attract attention for his efforts, he taught disadvantaged kids and young adults how to take better photos. He was a very generous man with his time.

Something else that always grabbed me was how polite he was to everyone. Okay so it's easy to keep a calm exterior when sitting with friends and family, even at work (most of the time). But occasionally something tips you over the edge, especially in and around the sometimes fractious situations that develop at football grounds. Not so Pete. He'd smile and laugh it off if anyone was unpleasant, turning the other cheek and disarming people with his humility.

I also covered the Crewe & Nantwich by-election, when Edward Timpson became the local MP, and then the 2010 General Election when the nation wondered if the Labour Party would take back the seat. On the sidelines capturing the political action behind the lens was Pete; me too on many of the campaign days. Unfortunately, the national media scrum also descended upon the towns, especially during three frantic by-election weeks in May 2008. The paparazzi boys (and girls) from London were like animals - quite literally. The snappers from the tabloids were particularly aggressive, out for themselves and happy to trample on anyone that got in their way.

Pete and I looked on one day, raising eyebrows to each other and stepping aside to grab another angle away from the mayhem. A photographer from one of the red tops elbowed Pete aside to get an uninterrupted line of sight to David Cameron who had arrived in Crewe to boost his candidate's chances of victory against Labour's Tamsin Dunwoody. Pete shrugged, and I suggested that we should head to High Street where the local *Guardian* office was situated. I knew they were en route there later, and access was awkward by car. We took a shortcut past Hops Belgian bar, and set up in a prime position before the political heavyweights arrived. There were no national hacks anywhere to be seen. Even then we talked football as we waited, the Alex always at the forefront of our minds.

I saw Pete at weddings, non-league football, charitable events and even the Town Sports at the Cumberland Arena in Crewe, and on the Barony fields in Nantwich, where he captured a great action picture of my youngest flying through the air in one of the sprint events. But it was always the Alex that made him really smile, stood there in all weathers wearing his unflattering "press" hi-vis top. He'd polish his glasses, check his lens, adjust his tripod and settle down ready to capture whatever the lads in red had to offer. And what a task that has been in recent seasons, dropping from the Championship and then suffering painful relegation and managerial uncertainty. He stuck around, and he deserved the Wembley triumphs as much as anyone. They were his days in the sun and he chronicled some amazing scenes that will adorn the walls of the club, cherished programmes and websites forever.

The phrases "too young to die" and "he was a great bloke" are bandied around too readily, but in each case the cap fitted perfectly. Pete was an outstanding gentleman, whether you'd met him once, twice or a hundred times at Alex matches or events around Cheshire. It was no surprise that so many people attended the memorial service at St. Mary's in Nantwich. His wife Pauline must have been immensely proud.

This is my tribute, a brief diversion from the *After Dario* story but one that highlights so well the fact that sometimes there are things much, much more important than football. The image of the Academy XI on the back page of this book was taken by him before the Walsall game in April 2013, a historic day for the club and one that he found very rewarding.

Pete Warburton; may he rest in peace.

AGAINST THE ODDS

To be perfectly honest, I think the majority of Alex fans thought that the 2013/14 season would be over before the end of February. We'd hit rock-bottom, dipped in and out of the relegation places, and could not stop conceding goals. The anger had passed, and there was a weary resignation that our number was up. Steve Davis had given it a crack, but League Two was calling us. So if ever the Crewe players were to hint that we might upset the bookies odds, it was fitting that they did it in style against our biggest rivals.

We all have games that stick in the memory, matches that tick every box and leave you wishing the moment had lasted forever. They are not necessarily play-off finals at Wembley, end-of-season promotion celebrations, or 5-0 romps when even the left-back scores a 30-yard screamer. For many reasons the away day at Port Vale was exceptional.

We have already covered the sad passing of Pete Warburton, but the Cheshire-Staffordshire derby engenders so many other emotions. For starters, I'd missed the last couple of Burslem dates - all of the tension, the excitement, the fear, the hatred and sometimes the elation. But the fixture had become so messy in recent seasons. Previous encounters had been chaos from start to finish, to the point where it was no longer enjoyable. We had been excluded from bars for no reason, abused in the streets, spat on and shunted along by the police when we only wanted to find a pint and a bite to eat.

In and around the ground was mayhem. Some of the younger Alex fans threw bottles at bar staff, so everyone was penalised and prevented from enjoying a few drinks. Post-match, as we left the ground, the Vale idiots (and I know, all clubs have them) had taken to hurling anything they could find, indiscriminately, at cars, coaches and innocent fans out for a day at the footy. It was torture, especially when we lost. But despite all that, I was hankering for the added spice that the fixture brings.

January and February brought moderate success for Crewe. We even beat Sheffield United 3-0 at Gresty Road. But a 1-3 defeat away at Brentford plunged us back into the relegation places. Still, I had a funny feeling that we might upset the odds against Vale. I couldn't resist it.

So for old times' sake I took the bus, the Arriva 20; back in the day it was the 320 PMT service connecting Crewe (as far as Leighton Hospital) to Hanley's bus depot. It was perfect, almost door-to-door as it slipped past Alsager, Kidsgrove, through Tunstall and into Burslem Square.

Along the way, we stopped at Church Lawton. A bunch of young teenage Alex lads jumped on and headed straight for the back seat. That was me, Bizza, Mike, Richard and Dave thirty five years earlier. Laughing and giggling at the lamest jokes, worrying about the match, wondering if we'd get our heads kicked in, whether our mums would find out that we'd gone to an away match when we had probably said that we were hanging around the village, playing football or watching Alsager Town.

The bus crawled up the incline, through Goldenhill, and then on past the first of the six towns that make up Stoke-on-Trent; suddenly the chatter from the back fell silent. Other supporters had boosted passenger numbers, and these were not Crewe fans. Furtive eyes darted up and down as the Alex posse tried to determine if the new arrivals were Vale fans. Then, as the trip neared its end, when the route up Scotia Road afforded views down terraced streets to the left, that most magical aspect of away-day travel came into play: floodlights appeared. Vale Park floodlights to be exact, proper old pylons reaching high into the sky, surveying what was left of the Potteries landscape of old.

There were pre-match beers in the Bulls Head pub off St. John's Square, a pasty to eat, and then a meet-up with a special lady outside the ground. This was also a day of research. As part of the Steve Davis biography project, I thought that it would be perfect sat alongside Mrs Davis, Betty, the manager's mum. I knew she was a keen supporter, but nothing could have prepared me for what lay ahead that afternoon. It was an unforgettable experience from the moment we grabbed programmes and made our way to the seats. And it was a truly family affair, as the Alex manager watched both of his footballing sons competing against each other, while the rest of the Davis clan was being entertained by the Vale directors.

The Alex end was bouncing. There was the now usual Crewe "crew" giving it large, youngish lads pointing and gesturing at Vale fans to the left in the Railway stand. The drums were out, and pre-match beers meant that the singing was free and easy - some tunes not particularly complementary to the hosts, as you'd expect! When the teams came out the volume increased again. Ben Garratt lapped it up, delighted and amazed to hear 1200 fans shouting his name. It was a massive test for the kid but he looked confident as he collected shots and crosses from his team mates. They all seemed up for it.

The Crewe goalkeeper needed to be on his toes. The early exchanges were quick and direct. Former Alex striker Tom Pope took the abuse from hostile Crewe fans, but he looked sharp. He unsettled nerves from the beginning. But it was Byron Moore, Mathias Pogba and Chuks Aneke who crafted the best early chances.

We saw yellow cards dished out as the referee tried to keep a lid on derby-day passions, but the tackles continued to fly in from all angles. It was frenetic. And when Moore lifted a cute cross towards the six-yard area, Pogba got stuck in. He barged through and nodded a header at goal; Vale cleared but the ball fell into a melee of players. Arms grabbed at shirts, legs swung, but Pogba reacted first. He bundled past his marker, toe-poking into the net. Easy! They just couldn't contain the big fella.

ABSOLUTE MAYHEM!

I left my seat with Pogba's first effort, and then ran down the steps to celebrate as the rebound was tucked away. I was ten yards from my original spot when everything calmed down. Alex fans went crazy. I staggered back and hugged Betty, and then screamed at a guy in front of us; proper football bonding in full flow. We were winning; more importantly we were winning in Burslem. And it's different against the Vale. It somehow means more, and it is twice as satisfying to see our lads also making the most of the moment. They went barmy. Davis and Neil Baker were no better. They wanted to join players and fans, but had to keep a respectful lid on their emotions as the Vale staff sulked in the dugout nearby.

Aneke should have doubled the lead before we'd settled. Then Pope rattled the Crewe bar, and Harry Davis cleared off the line just a few feet from the baying Alex fans. It was a party mood already, but one nutter went too far. He threw a red smoke bomb onto the pitch and found himself hauled unceremoniously from the seats. The stewards and police piled in. The temperature soared, and high up to our right in the Lorne Street stand a fight broke out; in the executive boxes!

It was a surreal scene. The police were still dealing with a number of Crewe fans behind the goal. Everyone looked up to the posh seats. A group from one executive box (Port Vale fans) were clambering over seating to get to another group stood outside the glass doors of an adjacent corporate area (Crewe fans). Punches landed, bodies tumbled and a roar went up as the rest of the ground watched on. The Vale Park security teams didn't know what to make of it. Fighting outside the sponsorship lounges; Betty was safer next to us! Yellow vests and padded jackets were soon running up the steps to intervene. Meanwhile, the match was heating up nicely.

Joe Davis was like a Tasmanian Devil. With his dad watching on, and his brother Harry keeping the Vale strikers quiet, the youngest of the Davis lads set about the Alex front men. He was wasting his time trying to topple Pogba. He was immovable. But Moore, Aneke and Bradden Inman all took a bashing. Davis (the Valiant) was fired up. A tough challenge on Moore earned the feisty defender a note in the referee's book. And then a crunching tackle on Aneke saw Alex fans foaming at the mouth.

OFF, OFF, OFF!

The majority chanted for a dismissal; except Betty. She stood up for the player as any grandma would. 'He didn't mean it,' she told the fella in front of us, 'he's a nice lad.'

But the lynch mob wanted blood. Vale boss Micky Adams decided that things were getting out of hand. He made two early substitutions; one of them saw Joe removed from the action.

The home side rallied, their supporters roared and Pope threatened yet again. They had the impetus as everyone took a breather at half time, but it was Crewe that grabbed another soon after the break. Matt Tootle enjoyed one of his mazy forays into opposition territory, skipped past a challenge, and then turned neatly as he threatened a cross. But his legs were taken by some desperate Vale defending.

PENALTY!

And it was just a few yards from jubilant Alex supporters who celebrated as though we had already scored. The stewards did their best to contain the situation, as over a hundred fans charged down to the barriers. They wanted to be close to the action. Aneke stayed cool and drilled a perfect spot kick to make it 2-0, and mass hysteria consumed the Crewe enclosure. It was fantastic, and the roof almost lifted when Inman dribbled, steadied and fired a beautiful shot into the bottom corner.

THREE-NIL TO THE RAILWAYMEN!

The singing and chanting was only topped for me when I turned to Betty in the final minutes of the match. 'One Steve Davis, there's only one Steve Davis' was repeated until the Alex manager waved to the travelling supporters. There she stood arms aloft, singing along. She even waved back at her son. Brilliant!

It's hardly worth mentioning Pope's consolation goal. He always scores against us, but even the Vale fans knew that their side was beaten. They were filing out in numbers by then, tossing "V" signs and bitter and jealous comments into the afternoon air as they went. The Alex end ignored them. We were too busy singing.

WE ARE STAYING UP!

The referee ended the contest and Alex gaffer Davis celebrated his 50th win in charge of the team. It was a very sweet victory. Apart from the desperately sad loss of Pete Warburton, the image that sticks in my mind is that of Davis and Neil Baker, stood on the pitch hugging each other in front of delirious Crewe supporters. It was magic.

The crazy thing about the win was that it didn't inspire the players to kick on and wrap up safety. Leaving Burslem that evening we had a healthy 34 points, still sixteen shy of the magical fifty that usually guaranteed safety. There was, however, real belief that we could now beat the drop.

***

The bookies didn't share our optimism. They are rarely wrong, and the clever money said that despite that epic Vale Park performance we were still going down. When we drew three and lost two of the next five games, many supporters started to believe them. If the Alex were to survive, it was going to be against the odds.

Thirty seven points on the board with nine games to go. It was a tall order. We needed four or five wins to guarantee survival, but the so-called "strugglers" around us had started winning games.

Two stunning away-day victories (at Gillingham and Crawley) should have seen the champagne corks popping, but they were punctuated by back-to-back home defeats. That is when I started to worry, especially as rock-bottom Notts County were one of the sides to beat us at Gresty Road. The mood changed considerably that evening. The boo-boys found their voices again, serious questions were asked and the blame game started in earnest.

At times, you do wonder whether Lady Luck is against you. When you're down, you're down, and other clubs fighting for points are more than happy to kick you as you lie wounded on the floor. Football has long been a dog-eat-dog industry, with little room for sentiment. The more cynical, wily managers will exploit every weakness to preserve their own status, or confirm promotion.

That's exactly what happened against Wolverhampton Wanderers at Gresty Road in early April. The Alex came under the cosh from the moment the referee started the match. Big, strong and powerful forwards hit our fragile rearguard early, firing shots from distance at every opportunity. Too often over the years I have watched lightweight Crewe Alexandra players call foul, look despairingly at the officials hoping for a decision to go in their favour. A shirt pull, shoulder barge or wayward elbow might have offended or injured, but in the rough-and-tumble of professional football the phrase "it's a man's game" has always carried weight. Unless a challenge draws blood or studs are shown, the officials plough on, blinkered vision intact. Nothing went our way!

Wolves won 2-0 that afternoon and secured promotion to the Championship. They were ruthless. Their fans flooded onto the pitch and celebrated in style. With four games to play we sat third bottom, with a shocking goal difference. That meant we had to end the season with a point more than our rivals to avoid the ignominy of relegation by the narrowest of margins. Still, the notion that the Alex could fall short was alien to me. It was unthinkable; but the black and white facts told a different tale.

Thankfully, Billy Waters heartened me in the midweek before the Good Friday game away at Shrewsbury. One of the younger squad members, he was featured on the official club website with upbeat quotes that reinforced my belief that we had enough to stay up. For me the academy has long been our saviour, and when other clubs hit the end-of-season wall, and injuries and suspensions rule many experienced pros out of contention, our kids stand head and shoulders above what the others have to offer.

At Shrewsbury they delivered. A high-pressure game, they kept their cool. When the team sheets were revealed ahead of the game, five of the starting eleven (Ben Garratt, Matt Tootle, Adam Dugdale, Liam Nolan and Byron Moore) came through the Alex academy at some point of their development. Casting an eye down the list of substitutes, a further four players (George Ray, Kelvin Mellor, AJ Leitch-Smith and Billy Waters) were home-grown. Nine from the 18-man matchday squad is impressive by any standards.

And what a day it was. The sun shone from the early hours, long before eager supporters set out for Shropshire. It was one of those feel-good mornings, when the journey ahead was no obstacle. Trains, cars, bicycles or even Shanks' Pony... as long as you got there it didn't matter how. I suspect that some would have crawled. This wasn't a relegation decider or a cup final, but it was a monumental six-pointer. Shrewsbury were second bottom, and the cross-county fixture would go a very long way towards deciding which of the two sides stayed in League One. For the losers, the trapdoor to the basement division would be creaking across the rest of the Easter weekend. Nobody wanted a draw, but I suspect that both managers would have taken the point if offered prior to kick-off.

Supporters, however, have a wholly different perspective. The points are important, of course they are. But when it comes to such emotional derby clashes, often seeing friends, family and work colleagues at loggerheads, the win is all-important. That this match came with relegation baggage merely added to the theatre. Tickets were snapped up; conversations at work were dominated by tactical considerations, whether the Alex would miss Chuks Aneke (suspended following a red card vs Wolves) and whether Shaun Miller would stick the knife in his former club's belly. Even the Shrews' gaffer added intrigue, as Michael Jackson (really) stepped out for Crewe in the 1992/93 season, making six appearances before moving to Bury on a free transfer. There were so many fascinating angles. It was another fabulous build-up that left everyone desperate for the action to begin.

The first arrivals in Shrewsbury took their places at riverside pubs just off the town centre as the temperature climbed into the early twenties. In bygone days the match was within walking distance, across the river at the old Gay Meadow ground. That was quaint, but as with so many clubs there was a desire to upgrade, move on, grandiose ideas and all. But everything starts in the town centre, and the bars and shops did a roaring trade as Alex fans piled off the train in considerable numbers.

There were rosy faces by midday, part alcohol-induced but also brought on by the fierce rays that reflected off the River Severn. It was a gorgeous setting, particularly beautiful by the waterside, the kind of day where best-laid plans are tossed aside and beery afternoons begin. Not on Good Friday, though. Not with football stakes riding so high. It was time to consider the lengthy trek to the new out-of-town stadium, a little over two miles from the centre.

There, nearly 1,500 Alex fans crammed into the north stand behind one of the goals. The magnitude of the game was emphasised by the numbers keen to roar the team on. It was the highest away gate since the Johnstone's Paint Trophy exodus to Wembley over a year earlier. Okay, so Shrewsbury remains one of those local rival clubs. It's a massive fixture, one that has carried resonance since the seventies when both clubs were Division Four (what is now League Two) bed fellows. This was the most important clash in years.

When the action started both sides set about each other as expected. Mathias Pogba was up for it, unleashing his inner bulldozer from the off. He threatened first, although former Alex man Miller was happy to lash shots at goal when anything came his way. Garratt, however, was a match for anything the Shrews threw at him.

For Crewe, the real Byron Moore stepped up, and with his contract elapsed at the end of the season it was good to see him prepared to give 100% to the cause. Town huffed and puffed, but for once the Alex house looked strong.

Mark Ellis was tested at the heart of defence, but he accepted every challenge with relish. If someone needed to stick a head in, he was there. There were a few industrial challenges, the odd shirt pull and a few well-timed elbows as he leaped with opposition strikers. But it was enough to help Garratt keep the Crewe goal intact.

That it was three lads brought to Crewe over the last eighteen months who scored mattered little. They celebrated as though their lives depended on it. Each player had good reason, as the records showed their combined names on the score sheet just eight times before the Shrewsbury match - Mathias Pogba (3), Uche Ikpeazu (3) and Anthony Grant (2).

Pogba's excuse for such a paltry return was that he'd been out of action for over half of the season. A very "unfriendly" July warm-up against Manchester United had seen the Alex striker come off worse in a 50:50 challenge. Since his return to action in January he'd looked off the pace. The man is built like the proverbial brick outhouse, so I suppose hauling his considerable bulk back to full fitness must be some task. So it was steady improvements as the season came to a climax. His comeback goal came away at Bradford (3-3), but at Shrewsbury he opened the Alex account with a brave and committed header from Jon Guthrie's corner.

The second came six minutes after the interval. Ikpeazu was a young man on-loan from Watford, prolific at youth level but struggling to adjust to senior football. The Alex pressed high up the pitch after the restart and from a neat ball to feet, Ikpeazu held firm on the edge of the six-yard area, shunted his aggressive marker back a few steps, steadied himself, rolled his man and whipped his foot around the ball to beat the static goalkeeper with a stunning strike into the top corner. It was straight from the training ground; Davis and Baker had encouraged him to try it. It worked. He was delighted.

And then to Grant, the midfield dynamo who does everything but score. A week earlier, when Wolves secured promotion at Gresty Road, he deservedly took the Alex "Man of the Match" accolade. He covered every inch of grass, winning tackles, drawing fouls and initiating good attacking moves. His overall game just lacked goals. His strike at Shrewsbury was only his third of the campaign, but what a contribution it was in the 89th minute.

Breaking up play in his usual robust fashion, for once Grant didn't leave a trailing leg to secure a free-kick. Instead, he powered forward. Shrewsbury were weary by now. Grant sensed their fatigue and drove forward into the centre circle. That was usually as far as his attacking runs took him. Everyone waited for a flick to the right, an angled pass across to Vadaine Oliver on the left, or even a shimmy, U-turn, or a time-wasting pass back to his defenders to use up a few vital seconds.

But no; Grant had a single-minded determination raging in his head. He was like a soldier prepared to charge at the enemy, his own safety the last thing on his mind. He continued apace, pushing the ball past two disbelieving Shrews' defenders praying for the final whistle. Where had this man got his energy from, they must have wondered? Then, as the penalty area opened up, the goalkeeper steadied himself and the massed ranks of Crewe fans packed behind the goal waited expectantly for a rising shot to rasp high above their heads and out of the stadium. How wrong we were. Grant looked up, adjusted his weight from one leg to the other, and then let fly. It wasn't a scorching top-corner net-buster; but he beat the goalkeeper.

GRANT SCORED!

The clock counted down, but oh-so slowly. Even winning 3-0 there were Alex supporters that could not help looking to the referee, desperate for that final whistle. Some of us have seen such leads surrendered in the dying minutes, and with the stakes so high such charity was not an option.

Then the tension was nudged up a few notches in injury time. Shrewsbury grabbed a goal back and the Alex contingent checked watches in unison. No way, it wasn't possible. Was it?

At times like this, the old ground by the river would have helped, a wayward kick sending the ball drifting down stream to waste a few seconds while the geezer in the coracle paddled furiously to retrieve the valuable piece of leather. But the referee was no mug and stopped his timepiece for a few seconds, determined to ensure that fair play prevailed. The home players hurried the restart, Davis and Bakes urged calm from the side lines, and then, after what seemed like an age, the Fat Lady sang her sweet, shrill tune to end a frantic and far-too even contest. Three-one flattered us, but the points mattered most.

The Crewe fans went daft, flinging themselves at the barriers but holding short of invading the pitch. The rest punched the air, ripped through a few choruses of "We Are Staying Up", while the more sedate applauded and recalled days when they too threw caution to the wind and danced about the terraces without a care in the world.

Then one very recognisable face came into focus. It was Dario Gradi, sat amongst the Alex fans enjoying the sunshine and beaming ear-to-ear. The club still runs through his veins, and accusations that he only bothers about developing the academy lads is way off the mark. He's often at away games, not part of the matchday travel with other club officials but driving to games himself. There are usually a handful of trainees with him, there to watch and learn alongside the master. He's a real football man; always has been and always will be. I am sure many supporters regret comments made over the years; that he had become out of touch; that he interfered too much; and that he was obsessed with Fair Play awards.

Maybe he was those things, but he was always doing what he thought was best for Crewe Alexandra. I flashed back to some of the more critical articles I penned for *The Sentinel* over the years, passages where I too called for change. I stand by those comments, as the time was right for him to move over, in 2007 and most definitely in 2011. Perhaps, but we should have gone easier on the man and not forced him into a corner. For the record, he had the last laugh that day. The players he had helped to develop, and still coached, had beaten Shrewsbury without picking up a single yellow card. The hosts earned three bookings. Who says that the good guys can't prosper?

Down on the touchline the "new" Alex management duo embraced, the players ran to salute the fans and the Shropshire hoards slipped out of the exits to make their way home. Their season was heading south. Perhaps the scoreline was distorted, but so what! None of the visitors cared about the matchday statistics, possession figures or the corner count. The fancy electronic display screamed the only numbers that mattered: Shrewsbury Town 1 Crewe Alexandra 3. With other results already in, details of the updated league table rippled through the away end; the Alex were out of the bottom four. Result! It was an awesome day out. The sunburn was soon forgotten, and survival was most definitely on the cards.

Most heartening was the route to victory that day. Teams scrapping for their lives are often forced to abandon neat routines and carefully orchestrated passages of play. Long-ball is the order of the day. The script is often straight-forward: heap pressure on the opposition, put them under the cosh as soon as the whistle sounds. Simple as that. Across the last twenty-odd years I'm struggling to remember when we did that. Perhaps under Gudjon Thordarson there was an edgy urgency, a more direct approach and a more sinister desire to spoil what the other side was trying to achieve. He was a man under pressure from day one. He needed to get results whatever, always under the cloud of longevity that hovered above courtesy of his predecessor. Now, under Davis, the softly-softly approach of Gradi and, briefly, Steve Holland was evident, but with added steel. We still needed the results, the vital points, but it was done with style.

The burning question for fans leaving the ground and those glued to radios, TV screens and social media updates was why? Not why had the Alex won, but why had we secured a third straight away win, when we'd taken just two points from the previous six home games? Without those vital victories on the road we would have been dead and buried; but what inspired those performances remained a mystery.

A popular theory was that the travelling support offered better vocal backing. The fans that formed the core away numbers were, largely speaking, die-hard loyalists. They would sing and support - win, lose or draw. They were critical, at times; they shared the same frustrations and vented their anger. The crucial difference being that their wrath was always kept under wraps until after the final whistle. Rarely during games did they barrack or criticise; that, across ninety minutes of combat, is when the players need encouragement the most. More often than not the two, three or four hundred travellers would sing, shout and applaud across each and every one of those minutes. It was all about the supporting the boys, and you had to take the rough with the smooth.

At home, within the Gresty Road confines that can hardly be compared to a caldron, too often the negativity bubbled over and intimidated those on the pitch. Some believe that professional footballers should be capable of ignoring comments from the stands, that their inflated salaries (even at League One level) should give them super powers, certainly enough confidence to play through pantomime jibes from supporters that watch through blinkers, too often seeing only the bad in their performances. Of the 4,000 average gates at Crewe, maybe one thousand pick and choose their games. They pay good money and they want to be entertained. The home ground is their fortress, so anything less than wins and the occasional draw are not good enough. Endure a losing sequence and the moaners can be heard above all voices.

But it's easy to be critical when times are hard. The 2013/14 season had been a nightmare, and many of the games from Christmas onwards had ended with disgruntled fans becoming increasingly vocal. We lost or drew far too many matches at home. At times it was embarrassing. In block "B" of the main stand, my spot alongside mates for the last decade, I often look down at rabid figures standing, pointing, shouting, gesticulating and stamping their feet when a player dares lose possession. It's comical. Sure the quality can be lacking, more so in some games when nothing goes our way. But I look at some supporters and they seem to view OTT protests as their duty. They lambast the manager when he doesn't make substitutions, then shower him with insults when the men introduced are not to their satisfaction. Of the tactical geniuses that I watched dish out astute observations across the most testing of seasons, not one has ever appeared at a fans' forum, nor have they ever dared offer their advice to the manager after a match in the bar.

So thank goodness for some spectacular victories on the road. We won six across 2013/14 and drew five. That's twenty three points, nearly half of the fifty required for safety in any given season. While it's great securing so many points away from home, we really should be enjoying better form at Gresty Road.

There were three games still to play; two of them were at home. It was cause for concern as we rounded the final corner of the season...

PRESTON

Only Crewe Alexandra could keep us hanging on until the last game of the season. After such a slick performance at Shrewsbury, a win over either Colchester (at home) or Bristol City (away) would have made things safe. So back-to-back 0-0 draws edged us closer but kept us scanning the other results and the league table right up until the final weekend. Our final match was Preston at home.

The serious worrying started at 7:45pm on Tuesday 29th April. There was a Champions' League semi-final sideshow playing on some household TVs, but my evening was spent nervously ironing, drinking copious amounts of tea and checking the Crawley Town vs Carlisle score every three minutes. Rock 'n' roll, eh? It was the Cumbrians' game in hand, the spanner in our works, the outcome of which could make the Preston finale even tenser. For one night only, the West Sussex side gained a few thousand extra fans from Crewe.

A win for Carlisle would have taken them to within one point of the Alex, with goal differences far too close for comfort. We didn't want any additional excitement clouding our end-of-season escape party!

Twenty minutes gone and it was still 0-0. I flicked to the BBC text commentary. The possession was 50:50 and that was concerning. Worryingly, Carlisle were still in it.

COME ON CRAWLEY!

SKY Sports News was no better; a quickie update from a roving reporter suggested that both sides had enjoyed chances. Then a corner for Carlisle; I shut my eyes, squinted, and then refreshed the page. Shot off target!

At half-time is was 0-0, which was okay, but surely Crawley would nick it? They didn't, it dragged on and on, free-kicks, corners, substitutions and still 0-0.

Towards the end it was like tracking an Alex game; painful. I decided to take the draw, leaving Carlisle needing a win away at Wolves (League One champions) on the final day. In the background the Champions' League semi-final was won at a canter by Real Madrid, leaving Bayern Munich smarting, so I checked the League One scores one last time. It was 0-0, all over, the league table reshuffled and the Alex were still in the driving seat. Our fate really was in our own hands.

The permutations were bonkers: two from Carlisle, Tranmere, the Alex or Notts County would be relegated by 5pm on Saturday 3rd May.

Here they were... the dreaded possibilities: if Crewe, Tranmere and Carlisle won then the Alex would survive. In fact, Notts County could then go down if they were defeated! If we all lost the Alex would remain in League One. If Crewe drew and Tranmere won then the Alex would slip down; the Carlisle result would be irrelevant unless they hammered Wolves (unlikely, we hoped). If Crewe drew, Tranmere did similar and Carlisle won, we would survive; the "Scousers" from Birkenhead might drop out if the Brunton Park boys went goal crazy (again, unlikely). But, if Preston beat us, Tranmere lost and Carlisle won, well, it would hinge on how many those pesky Cumbrians won by and how many we conceded. Phew! Did you follow all that?

Okay, I can boil that ridiculous ramble down to five words...

THE ALEX NEEDED TO WIN!

I love getting carried away with football. It's just a game, of course it is, but for so much of every year it is a force that I cannot shake off. The next opponent matters to me; I need to check the league table two, three and four times each week; there's always the goal difference to worry about; player injuries concern me; and I fuss over weather forecasts in case the elements should have an adverse effect on the next match. It's ridiculous. But some games are undeniably momentous.

Preston at home on the final day of the season was one of those occasions. It was (brace yourself, it is cliché time) our cup final; it was a one-off, an event that would affect our standing in the English pyramid. The result would have financial implications, players would base contract negotiations on it, and fans would be left with a small slice of history that would be etched on their footballing memories forever.

From Wednesday afternoon I tried to switch off. Now that can be hard to achieve at work, as 50% of those dotted around the factory have Alex affiliations. Even the others, those Premier League armchair supporters that lap up the SKY and BT Sports subscriptions also have a soft spot for Crewe.

'Can we stay up then?' was asked three hundred and forty seven times. I kid you not. I never exaggerate. Of course, I always reply in the positive and maintain that survival was a formality, but then for weeks I had been saying we would have safety wrapped up before we travelled to Shrewsbury. I only dismissed the fanciful notion of another surge up the table into that sixth play-off spot in early April. I know... deranged!

So I made it to Saturday exhausted, all talked out and my brain frazzled with over-analysis. Every sports bulletin had highlighted the relegation candidates, the exciting showdown at the foot of League One and the prospect of bumper gates for those who survived as the mighty Birmingham looked likely to drop down from the Championship. The stakes were certainly high. We all wanted the higher standard, despite the tough season we had endured. It tested us and it was worth it.

As many had pointed out during the build-up to matchday, we had enjoyed the highs of Wembley in very recent history; now it was time for the supporters to step up and back Davis and his players 100%.

It looked promising as I wandered through town. Eager punters clutched optimistic betting slips. Replica tops and scarves were out in force. A red tide of enthusiasm, hope and expectation was being drawn towards Gresty Road. Even one of the market traders called me over. 'Hope you do it,' he said, adding 'I bloody hate that Tranmere lot.' He was an Evertonian!

Down Edleston Road I wandered, still wondering what the day would bring, past the pubs and on to the train station. I met the lads as they arrived, yet more miles covered by them for the Alex cause. There was Andy from Nuneaton, Alan from Coventry, Ray and Marie making an easier trip from Alsager. Everyone wore glazed expressions, hiding the fear and putting on brave faces.

BEER O'CLOCK!

We made our way to the first stop, the excellent bottle bar called Beer Dock. Alex fans were everywhere along the route, but there was a sizeable invasion from Preston. Lilywhite tops strutted proudly up and down Nantwich Road - in the Corner Bar, Seven, Tonic and Last Orders. Bouncers doubled up on each doorway, although everything suggested a light-hearted afternoon of friendly banter. And it was all good-natured, but deep down we knew there was a job to be done. Securing either third or fourth spot would mean home advantage in the second leg of the play-off semi for Preston. So they needed a result to keep Leyton Orient and Rotherham at bay. This was never going to be a romp for Crewe, but several of their fans wished us luck as we walked down the street. They, like most supporters around the country, had the Alex as one of their "other" teams. And of the clubs at the bottom, they wanted us to survive.

The pre-match beers were essential. A few to calm the nerves went down very easily and an extended session was on the cards by 2:00pm. But there was too much riding on the match. We needed to be focused, to watch every moment, keep tabs on other scores and encourage the lads on the pitch at every opportunity. We grabbed another at the Brunnie, also wall-to-wall with Preston lads. The Championship games were showing on the big screens all around the pub, and they cheered as rivals Blackpool conceded, and booed when Birmingham avoided the drop with almost the last touch of the game.

Then, at 2.35pm, we headed to the ground, uncharacteristically early, as we were desperate for the game to start, keen to soak up every last detail and be properly ready for what lay ahead. For the umpteenth time in our supporting lives, we were like little kids; excited, nervous, desperate to unwrap the present of League One survival that was now in touching distance.

Walking through those turnstiles, and then up the concrete steps and onto the vast concourse set the butterflies loose. The tension was palpable, on a par with the edgiest matches in our recent history. I stalled to check if the lads were with me, ready to take our places in the stand. They were, and all around were other familiar faces; men, women and kids that have walked past us a thousand times, accidentally brushed us aside in rushed moments, acknowledged us, said hello or shared highs and lows before, during and after games. It's what being part of a modest club is all about. They are just people, fellow supporters, holding hot dogs, teas and coffees, and carefully folded programmes. They were getting ready for the ninety minutes that stretched out before us, now less than a quarter of an hour away. There were expressions of hope, trepidation and determination, but genuine belief that we were going to do it.

ONWARDS AND UPWARDS...

It was ridiculously early. We never get in until 2.55pm. My catalogue of missed kick-offs grows by the season; but not against Preston. There was no way we were going to be late. Up we went, noise intensifying with each stride, the dull roar of football fans revving up for the main attraction. But there was still the team sheet to discuss. The manager had stayed loyal to the lads who had secured a point away at Bristol City the previous Saturday. I liked that; it would have meant a lot to those players. That draw was enough to take us into the final weekend still in control of our own destiny. They deserved a chance to lap up the glory. Chuks Aneke returned to the bench following his three-match suspension; he would be chomping at the bit, desperate to sign-off a great season away from his host club Arsenal. So we now knew who would be starting the game.

We emerged from the shadows to a pool of sunshine that lit up the pitch like a gladiators' arena. The visiting hordes on the far side cut an impressive sight. Their seating areas were already packed, just a handful of seats vacant. White and green smoke snaked high above their enclosures as the first flares were let off. They were ready; singing, drumming, some in fancy dress, some with tops off, watching balloons bob up and down, and then floating to the rafters above. The essential beach ball also pinged from back to front, the head tennis game kept alive by stewards keen to maintain the carnival mood. It was the kind of away-day party we'd enjoyed many times ourselves over the years.

The Gresty Road end looked equally wired. It wasn't full, but not far from it. Many of its residents were still supping in the Alexandra Suite next door, tucked away beneath the sumptuously named Whitby Morrison Ice Cream Van Stand (Popside). But they were slowly filtering in, past the food kiosk, out into bright light of battle. They all cast an eye left, some adding a raised finger for good measure, a welcome and a warning to the Preston lads giving it large by the police box. The TV cameras didn't catch that, but they did capture the plumes of red smoke that added to the already charged atmosphere. A BBC North West crew sat at the other end of the stand, popping questions to supporters ahead of the action. They were filming the drama for the *Late Kick-Off* programme due to be screened the following Monday, a minute-by-minute documentary piece of the final day emotions that affected two of the region's clubs.

All around the colour was fabulous. Red and white predominantly, but plenty of obscure shades and combinations; second and third kits worn in seasons past by both sets of fans. Even our lofty perch towards the back of block "B" was filling up. Strangers, long-time-no-seers, anyone and everyone keen to be part of another landmark game. Expectancy rippled across the massed bodies that would later be declared as a bumper 7,458 attendance. It was almost game time.

FIVE MINUTES TO KICK-OFF!

We had one final pleasure before the action. Our much-missed friend, Mike Lazenby, was also with us. At least his mum and dad were, Christine and Roger taking in their annual game to honour his memory. We hugged, kissed and shook hands. It was a touching moment; we were lucky to be there, ready to watch the team that had drawn Mike from miles away, season after season, even in the final days when he was ill. He was gone but somehow sat beside us. Also there were Marie, Ray, Paul, Margaret, my old mate Higgy from Alsager, then Mossy and his young lad Owen, signed in and present, all part of that extended Alex family, all wanting the same thing.

When the ball rolled off the centre-spot we knew it was real. No turning back. Soon we'd know whether it was Sheffield United, Coventry, Port Vale and Bristol City the following season, or maybe Newport, Accrington, Cheltenham and Exeter. We wanted trips to cities, fabulous days out and the chance to claim big scalps. The bean counters saw things differently; they demanded success. They needed tills to ring. If we failed, home crowds could perhaps dip by one thousand and more. That would mean lower incomes and less chance to recruit better players. It wasn't an option. Now it really was game on.

The first action wasn't at Gresty Road though. On an afternoon of such significance there was no chance that supporters would keep clear of radios and mobile phones. What Tranmere and Carlisle were doing was all-important. It could influence how Davis set up the side late on as the clock wound down. So we all tuned in, bobbed heads over shoulders as others flashed devices, and furtively checked our own favourite streams of footy information.

Wolves smashed an early one past Carlisle. Brilliant! Not unexpected, but far better to have them out of the picture. Prenton Park was the main worry. So hearing that Tranmere had taken the lead after seven minutes set hearts fluttering. Those informative but awful real-time league tables didn't help matters. The Alex slipped into the virtual bottom four; a point against Preston was no longer enough. I looked around, and twenty years ago the cigarettes would have come out. Now it was fingernails being chewed to their stumps. As things stood, we were going down!

Step forward Adam Dugdale. A man who had endured much personal pain over recent years, he joined the attack when the Alex won a corner on ten minutes. Now we don't usually get too excited about set pieces. Despite having a few sizeable units on board, with height and power throughout the team, the ball rarely hits the back of the net from corners. So when Jon Guthrie shuffled, signalled and swung his foot at the ball there was no eager anticipation of a goal. But Duggy changed all that. He leapt high, arms flaying to keep his marker down.

BOOM!

His header had *"no returns welcome"* etched on the ball. What a time to grab his first Alex goal in two years! He raced away, brushing aside team mates, pumping his fist at the Crewe fans in the main stand. *"1-0 to The Railwaymen"* was sung before he completed his celebrations. The league table reshuffled. It looked bloody fabulous. We were back in control.

Then it was time to check out the other games. Carlisle went two goals down at Molineux; so goodnight to them. And the lads on the Wirral saw red, losing a man just after the half hour. In fact, the Tranmere player dismissed was Junior Brown. He never played for the Alex, but he was born in Crewe. Now they would have to defend for their lives, to preserve their precious lead. That was always a dodgy tactic, as the Alex knew all too well.

But Crewe pressed on, hungry for goalmouth chances. Byron Moore, Mathias Pogba and Uche Ikpeazu all buzzed, battered and barged through North End's rearguard. They just couldn't find the all-important second goal. It wasn't one-way traffic but we started to boss the match; until about 35 minutes in. Then Preston stepped up a gear and looked as though they wanted it more. They were already in the play-offs, but 2,200 PNE supporters hadn't come to watch their side collapse. They needed to prepare for the final push and map out a route to Wembley. And they did, probing deep and testing young Ben Garratt on a few occasions. Down below the Alex manager acted fast. It was too soon for changes but he looked to the twelfth man. Davis turned and conducted the crowd, determined to whip everyone into frenzied support. He wanted us on side. We responded, the main stand immediately rocking to *"Alex, Alex..."* as even the most timid sang along. This was a team effort more than ever. The "cup final" was going to plan and we had one hand on the trophy. Dropping it was not an option.

Quite why we dashed for a half-time bevvy I don't know. Perhaps it was nerves, or maybe a desire to relive the old ritual that was once the norm (in our younger days). In reality it meant another toilet break before heading back for the second half. The tepid lager didn't break Preston's flow, however, and the restart mirrored the tail-end of the first period. They fancied it, and could still take something from the game - if not win it. There were a few heart-in-mouth moments as they pressed, deeper and deeper into the Alex half. But then it stopped. The formidable Ikpeazu drove hard down the right side of the Preston area, and the Watford loanee destroyed his marker - quite literally. He reached the by-line, dragged the ball back and fed Pogba. The big fella thumped it past the 'keeper and it ricocheted off a despairing defender's leg.

GOAL!

This time we jumped into the air, all worries tossed aside in a fleeting moment. The main stand was a jumbled mass of uncontrolled movements, arms and legs like a writhing game of Twister! Everyone had their own celebration.

WE ARE STAYING UP!

I turned to Ray as my feet left the floor, arms outstretched, and landed in a pile, hugging him in that awkward footy-fan manner, only releasing as we realised that his Mrs was watching. But we didn't care. It was our moment. It was Crewe's moment. There was madness everywhere. We were 2-0 up and cruising.

Across the pitch the Preston army fell silent. To our left the Gresty Road end rocked. I watched a dad lift his young son high into the air so that he could see the other players peeling away to mob the goal scorer. It was a memory that would last his lifetime. Pogba raced to the technical area where Davis and Bakes were already in raptures. The team spirit was overflowing.

Then we started to get cocky. There were no olés but at 2-0 we passed the ball like Barcelona. There was added zip, and the players oozed belief. We could keep the ball if we wanted. Less than ten minutes to go and Bradford equalised at Tranmere. I can only imagine the hurt their supporters were feeling. We'd been there, and we didn't want it again. Now we could see the finishing line. A few showboat passes put smiles on faces, Davis barked orders to keep things tight, but then news filtered through of Bradford's second goal. Now Tranmere were losing, and we were two up. It was time to party!

Those final minutes didn't bother me. It was our day. Even the 90th minute consolation goal for Preston didn't ruin the mood. Okay, so we double-checked that Tranmere were still trailing and that Carlisle hadn't started the most miraculous of comebacks, but there was no sweat lost on row FF. The first home win since Saturday 1st February was pulling into the station right on time. Nobody was leaving the ground, but hundreds were gathering down by the advertising barriers below. I really fancied it and headed down the steps. I would meet the lads in the bar after. For the next ten minutes I would become a teenager again. I hadn't been an invader for many years, and I wanted to grab some in-the-thick-of-it photos.

The referee didn't quite have the whistle to his lips when I made my move. But it was coming; it was only seconds away as I stood there and smiled at a steward who knew exactly what was about to happen. The game was over, there was no point prolonging the situation, and we wanted to get onto the pitch. Wolves had done it two weeks earlier, rubbing their fabulous promotion in our faces as they celebrated all over our hallowed turf. Now it was our turn. There was polite applause from most of the main stand, but I joined the rebellious Gresty Road end crew and raced to celebrate with our players. I legged it, a 48-year-old man cutting though bodies as though I was sixteen again (just with dodgy knees). It was mayhem as everyone surged over the touchline and out towards the centre circle where dazed footballers were still coming to terms with what had just happened. Cameras popped and mobile phones captured the stampede on video; it would be uploaded later and enjoyed again and again.

The pitch wasn't important; they re-seed it every summer. So why stop the fans having their moment out on playing surface? There was a brief flurry of steward activity, but I was already slapping Mark Ellis on the back. A thousand Alex fans were alongside and behind me, pounding the grass, showing more pace than some of the tired legs had in the dying minutes of the match. We reached our heroes before the final notes left the official's whistle. Those majestic men in red were jubilant. They had delivered. It was a combined effort of course, and they danced and sang "We Are Staying Up" with the ecstatic supporters who flocked around them. Those few minutes, shared with players that had been questioned, applauded and derided during previous games were the best of a miserable nine months. That 2-1 victory made everything alright. The dross was forgotten, we could plan the next year of our lives, selecting which away games to squeeze in around family commitments. That sounds so sad, but it's been the reality for so long. Life revolves around football for so many people; some just choose to deny it.

A little later the post-match scenes in the main bar were remarkable, but the atmosphere was definitely tinged with relief. The room was packed. Everyone wanted to see the elation on players' and management faces, especially the gaffer's. It was the end of three memorable seasons for Davis. He didn't look relieved as he walked through the supporters at about 5.25pm; he looked drained, a physical wreck despite his smart suit and beaming smile. He posed willingly, as he always does, for a photo with the lads and Mike's mum and dad.

It was a stylish sign-off to a torrid nine months. Now Davis could plan, build, assess and plot his and the club's next moves. Few would have begrudged him a few weeks off, and I suspect that his wife, Gaynor, was more than ready for the break. She, more so than any of us, will have witnessed each twist, turn, peak and trough across the most turbulent spell of what was still only a brief managerial career at Crewe. He not only survived the toughest of seasons, he ultimately prospered completely against the odds.

Trying to convey how important football is to some people is almost impossible. Thousands attend to enjoy good play, watch occasional flashes of brilliance and ride the roller-coaster highs. But others live for it. They attend whatever the game's significance. They tune in to every broadcast and pore over and over even the briefest snippets in newspapers and magazines. When the Alex lose it hurts. If the players and manager do not reflect that pain there is something wrong, and the football-family bonds weaken - often to breaking point. But when blood and guts are spilled, when those heroes give us 100% and do anything and everything to secure the win that guarantees survival, well, sharing that delirium is all part of the experience. There is no better sight than fans, players and management cavorting like children. There's a shared satisfaction and a sense of achievement as everyone kisses the collective badge. Davis pulled it off that day. He took the crowd with him. Preston never had a chance. If only you could bottle it!

So was this better than any Championship survival of, say, 1999, 2000 or 2005? I'd like to say yes, despite the quality being considerably lower. There were so many factors that, in my opinion, made this the greatest of escapes. Her Majesty would no doubt have labelled it a *Season Horribilis!* It had everything, from a decent pre-season that brought Manchester United and Blackburn Rovers to Gresty Road, to another high-profile player sale that would, ultimately, unsettle the side and leave us wanting in midfield. Then the nightmare that was Cornwall, the club's good name dragged through the mud. With that thankfully resolved by mid-November, the gaffer then had issues with several disruptive players. He must have wondered what he'd done wrong in a previous life. There was a clear-out of sorts, head-to-head confrontations to hammer things out, and then injuries and suspensions to make life even harder for the beleaguered management team. That the club limped on and didn't get marooned at the foot of the table is astonishing. There were times when all looked lost, but a spirited display at Vale Park in February gave everyone hope, and an unexpected but very welcome string of away wins finally saved the day.

Davis et al breathed a mighty sigh of relief. It was dramatic. As many pointed out it wouldn't be the same if the Alex didn't keep us guessing until the last minute. We'll look back at this in a few seasons and wonder how on earth Davis pulled it off.

ONGOING LEGACY

Thankfully, *After Dario* was completed with the season done and dusted. The Preston game allowed me to wrap things up. Nothing was left hanging. We won, relegation was avoided and Steve Davis told us that survival against the odds was without doubt his best achievement to date as manager of Crewe Alexandra. Everyone at the club could plan for another third-tier season.

What struck me in the final weeks of writing this text was that the title "After Dario" still referred to our former manager. Okay, so the cover picture shows who is now driving the team forward. Gradi sits in the background while Davis is the dominant force, the one who dictates how the first team shapes up and how we play. That, I suppose, is the point, that although we're some way down the line after the great man stepped aside he is still there, a significant presence and source of advice. There is very little that he has not seen, done or encountered in the three divisions outside of the Premier League. You cannot help but celebrate that experience, especially when he arrives fresh-faced for duty each day at Reaseheath.

So for me Davis is shaping an ongoing legacy; he is following on, maintaining and tweaking something created by Gradi, John Bowler and a host of coaches and dedicated back-room staff. That sounds bizarre, as "legacy" is normally something that has been handed down and passed on. Davis has not moved on, yet, but he has undoubtedly added to the DNA at Gresty Road. His stamp is most evident, but at the core of everything is youth. That has to be the case.

At Crewe anyone who takes up the challenge to play, manage or work for the club must embrace what has gone before and commit to upholding its values. Davis does all that, and as we witnessed at home to Walsall in 2013, he took the whole youth scenario to its ultimate conclusion. He was brave, something acknowledged by his number two, Neil Baker, who was quoted on the club website crewealex.net: 'We love to give our home grown players a chance. If they are good enough to play at this level then we will play them. The manager has always been willing to throw them in at the deep end and has probably been braver than even Dario would have been with some of them.'

But there's also a cold and calculated streak about Davis. He was a successful player and knows that harsh decisions need to be made. He cannot and will not be everyone's friend. He uses the academy players to the max because they are good enough, not because he feels the need to pander to his paymasters. But anyone who falls short must look out. Two surprising departures at the end of the 2013/14 season were AJ Leitch-Smith and Kelvin Mellor. This is perhaps where Davis and Gradi differ. Under the previous regime I believe that they would have been given another season. That is fine, very loyal and shows great determination to continue developing players that have been at the club for years. But it doesn't progress the squad. It remains adequate, if not a little stale. The ambitious Davis wants more than that.

As for others in the squad, in particular those not schooled at Crewe, there was no messing around when the most recent season was completed. The "released" list issued soon after the final game was severe. Included were Mark Ellis, Steve Phillips and Abdul Osman, all solid professionals but unlikely to improve or help take the club further the following season. Football can be an unforgiving business.

I believe that we will see fewer bought-in players at Crewe as we move forward. It's a huge gamble investing in largely unknown quantities. There's often an upfront fee, two or three years of wages (and at much higher salaries than those paid to recent academy graduates) and there is no guarantee that the players concerned will adapt to the Crewe way of life. It is, after all, a unique club that does not suit everyone, especially wisened footballers who sometimes think that they know better than the manager. Although many factors hampered Davis' third season, many felt that the recruitment of players could and should have been better after Luke Murphy departed. Davis acknowledged that, but also relishes the opportunity to put things right.

Even Gradi backed Davis to learn from errors of judgement. 'We haven't paid for our mistakes; the trick now is not to make the same mistakes. I think more significant than any off-field problems, was that some of the players we brought in last summer didn't live up to expectations,' he told *The Crewe Chronicle*. Gradi was shouldering some of the responsibility. The reference to "we" was most revealing. For most of the first part of the torrid 2013/14 campaign all fingers pointed at Davis. He was responsible for bringing in those fresh faces, but Gradi, the board and the other coaches had all signed off the deals. It's a team effort at Crewe, and although many often feel that Gradi is the dominant force (even now) I believe that there is a fantastic collective vibe running through the club, from Reaseheath to the offices at Gresty Road. You only have to look at the length of service of many of its employees to realise how much they all cherish being part of a feel-good, close-knit operation. It's certainly the envy of everyone who visits and spends time at its facilities.

Although it's a modest set-up compared to many clubs, nobody stands still. It's not always apparent, but there's a genuine desire to keep improving, certainly to avoid making the same mistakes. In particular, the whole process of recruitment from elsewhere and progression from the academy needs to be carefully managed. As such, John Bowler made some fascinating observations. Behind the scenes, the academy needs to 'highlight the positions where the club is weak' he told me. That translates to ensuring that another one or two midfielders are ready next time we are forced to make quick sales over consecutive seasons. A simple traffic light system of red, amber and green will track the players coming through. When the red alert sounds then the coaches and scouts need to react, perhaps cast the net further and plug the gaps that the academy cannot fill immediately. He revealed that everyone is 'fully supportive' of the system.

Those "gaps" will not be filled using the transfer market. Instead, the "system" will prosper using loan players to the club's advantage. The contacts that Davis and Gradi have built up will also prove priceless. And they will be vital links with the biggest clubs in England: Arsenal (Steve Bould), Man City (kick-started by David Platt), Liverpool (Neil Critchley) and Chelsea (Steve Holland); all involve former players, coaches and close friends. It would be mad if we did not make full use of such resources.

It's important to note, however, that players will not be brought to Crewe for the sake of it. Preference will always be given to the local boys, if they hit the required standard. Putting the final touches to these pages I noticed the list of academy scholars that had been offered professional contracts. In the summer of 2014 it was six players. Other years have seen even greater numbers. For the record they are: Fraser Murdock, Callum Saunders, James Jones, James Baillie, Perry Ng and Callum Pritchard-Ellis. They all signed up because they know that they will be well represented, coached properly and introduced to the matchday squad when they are ready.

We wish them well, look forward to watching them excel and, with a heavy heart, eventually see them fly the Alex nest when one of the Premiership clubs tempts us and them with pieces of gold. I just hope that we get to "enjoy" our players for two or three full seasons.

The message is simple: in our youth we trust. For the foreseeable future that will be the case, and if I'm honest our current standing in level three of the English game is ideal for the development of our young players.

In the basement division more of them would get the chance to play, just as the tricky trio of Powell, Westwood and Murphy did in 2011/12. But I'd love to think that we will never drop below League One again, maybe pushing for the play-off positions once more so that another day in the Wembley sun could turn daydreams into Championship reality. That would be fabulous, and better still if Davis could achieve it with a solid core of home-grown players at its heart.

The Crewe system is like a perpetual motion machine, something ahead of its time that others have tried and failed to replicate. The fact that it works and continues to give young players opportunities in the professional game is its unique selling point. One touching moment came with a high profile ex-Premier League player announcing that his son would be joining the Alex academy. At the final game of 2013/14, at home to Preston, Cassius Cisse, son of former Liverpool, Marseille, Lazio and France star striker Djibril, took part in a demonstration game put on for youngsters before kick-off. His mum, Jude, wrote online: 'It was an extremely tough decision to help him make with him being so young and the most important factor is that he enjoys it. As a result Cassius made HIS choice to sign with Crewe Alex.' Such confidence in what Crewe has to offer bodes well for subsequent years. Liverpool, Manchester United and Everton were overlooked because the Alex offers a more intimate, personal touch, plus a far greater chance of advancement to the first team.

I'm still incredibly proud that my football allegiances are firmly with Crewe Alexandra. We have never bought success, we still try to play an attractive blend of football, and the stadium is still situated in the heart of one of the town's original communities. Gradi is responsible for much of the above. He's still there. He is still passionate about our club. His part in the legacy will last forever.

There will be change over the coming years, and as supporters we must accept that. Gradi nurtured, improved and encouraged the young Steve Davis to fly the nest as a player. Years later he once again set him free; this time with the keys to the club. He always did empower people. He's a teacher and loves seeing his pupils flourish.

Davis is the present and future of Crewe Alexandra, although he will surely move on. Whether he stays three months into the new season, three years or does go on to top Gradi's amazing tenure remains to be seen. By summer 2014, he had just completed two and a half seasons in charge. Looking at the length of service across the leagues I noticed a crazy statistic: only fourteen men (out of 92) had served longer than him.

The turnover of managers is startling. It speaks volumes of the insatiable demand for success at all levels.

There will never be another "Dario" and we should not look to Davis to replace the man in our hearts. He is very different. We need to enjoy what he brings to our club; and no matter how long it lasts I'll be here to witness it, as will several thousand Alex supporters who have the club entwined in their lives. Directors, managers, coaches and certainly players come and go. The fans, by and large, stick around and support forever.

My only caveat is that subsequent managers share the same vision and commitment to the philosophy that has served our club so well for over thirty years. Long may it continue…

ACKNOWLEDGEMENTS

As ever, there are so many people to thank. Little nuggets of information, handy tips and invaluable advice have all helped me to complete this project. So, in no particular order, much appreciation to the following: Ray Belcher, Andy Howarth, Karen Bingham, Simon Welch, Mark Potts, Tony Marks, Andy Scoffin, Glen Battams, Rob Wilson, Adam Breeze, Peter Morse and Colin Higginson.

Elsewhere, with social media such a powerful tool nowadays, credit must go to the many people who swapped notes, generated ideas and threads, dropped reminders and put me straight a few times. So I sincerely hope that I have captured all of the names. Again, in no particular order: Matt Owen, Ant Critchley, Adam Gray, Steve Hatton, Martin Dunning, Julie Warren, David Gallagher, Jim Wiltshire, Toby Robinson, Ian Conder, Stuart Grimley, Steve Davies, Colin Higginson, Trevor Griffiths, Shaun Rogers, Paul Howarth, Garrett Sandeen, Andrew Copeland, Kev Graham, Dave Egerton, Paul Blakeman, Chris Simpson, Richard Banks, Andrew Willavoys, Phil Bedford, Ian Affleck, Tim Tantram, Jim Lawrence, Duncan Burrow, Shaun Edwards, Jack Jones, Peter Robinson Smith, Andy McIntyre, Warren Ruscoe, Steve Johnson, Steve Bennett, Chris Thompson, Ben Breeze, Gary Cliffe and Graham McGarry. And to anyone I might have forgotten, although that hardly makes up for missing you out!